Hons
(Dulles)

Innovative Strategies for Unlocking Difficult Children

Written by:
Robert P. Bowman, Ph.D.,
Tom Carr, M.S.,
Kathy Cooper M.S.W.,
Ron Miles, Ph.D.,
Tommie Toner, M.Ed.

D1413834

© 1998 by
YouthLight, Inc.
Chapin, SC 29036

All rights reserved.
One copy of the Activities may be made for the express purpose of
providing the material to a child. Other reproductions can not be made
without written permission.

Cover Design by Paul Neuburger
Illustrations by Walt Lardner
Project Layout by Elizabeth Madden
Project Editing by Melissa White

ISBN 1-889636-08-8

Library of Congress

10 9 8 7 6 5 4 3 2
Printed in the United States of America

Table of Contents

I. Introduction

The Nature of the "Difficult" Child 1
Things to Remember About Difficult Students 2
"High Risk" vs. "Difficult" Children 3
Underlying Causes of Difficult Behavior 4

II. Managing the "Difficult Classroom" 5

The Difficult Classroom 6
Ten Ways to Quiet a Classroom 9
Survival Skills for the Classroom Teacher 10
Activity: "Center Time" 11
Activity: "Cooperation Game" 12
Activity: "Connecting" 13
Encouraging Student Involvement...14
Thirty-One Incentive Plans 15
Tips for Surviving a "Difficult Classroom" 22
Problem-Solving Steps for Children 22
Using Negotiation in Child-Teacher Conflicts 23
Interventions When the Student's Need Is Power.....................................24
Improving Students' Social Skills 26
Crisis Management 27
The Process of Crisis Management 28
Immediate Post-Trauma Debriefing 29
Parent Coupon Booklet 30

III. Focus on Attention Seekers 31

Helpful Hints for Dealing with "Attention Seekers"...............................32
ADD/ADHD 33
Teaching Students with Attention Deficit Disorder 34
"Gossipers/Tattlers" 36
Helpful Hints for Dealing with "Gossipers" and "Tattlers" 37
Strategies for Dealing with Tattling 38
"SHARE" With Attention-Seeking Students 43
Activity: "Refuse the Gossip Game" 44
Activity: "GOSSIP" 45
Activity: "No Fighting Game" 46
Activity: "Solving Problems By Myself"...48
Activity: "Solving Problems Baseball Game" 50
Activity: "Line It Up" 52
Activity: "Go Fishing" 53
Activity: "Crater Cross" 55
Activity: "Talking Behind Your Back" 56
Activity: "Duck, Duck Friend" 57

Activity: "What I Can Do Book" 58
Activity: "Musical Dress Up" 59
Activity: "Musical Moves" 60
"Class Clowns" 61
Helpful Hints for Dealing with "Class Clowns" 62
Activity: "The Clown Game" 63
Activity: "Attention Circles" 64

IV. Focus on Manipulators 65

"Truth Benders" 66
Helpful Hints for Dealing with "Truth Benders" 68
Activity: "Lies" 69
Activity: "What if?" 70
Activity: "Yes or No Game" 71
Activity: "Shoot the Hoop" 72
Activity: "Stick Together" 73
"Game Players" 74
Becoming Game-Wise 76
Restructuring Student "Games" 78
Activity: "Match It Up" 79
Activity: "Stop the Behavior Game" 80

V. Focus on Hostile/Aggressive Students 81

Nine Tips on Being Angry and Fighting Fair 82
How to Handle Conflicts Constructively 83
Student Responses for Conflict Resolution 84
Building a Cooperative Community 85
Teaching Students Appropriate Social Skills 86
Enabling Students to Communicate Effectively 88
Activity: "Sunshine Game" 94
Activity: "Monster Game" 95
Activity: "Clowning Around Game" 96
Encouraging Students to Become Helpers 97
Unique Strategies for Dealing with the Angry/Aggressive Student 98
Suggestions for Handling Hostility in Students 101
Plans for Dealing with the Extreme Hostile Student 103
"Sherman Tanks" 104
Television Violence 108
Activity: "Non-Violent Alternatives to Fighting" 109
Activity: "Anger Pictures" 110
"Snipers" 111
Helpful Hints for Dealing with "Snipers" 113
Activity: "Chip Away" 114
Activity: "Home Run City" 116
"Exploders" 117
Helpful Hints for Dealing with "Exploders" 120

Activity: "Deflate the Teaser's Balloon" 121
"DEFLATE" Your Anger 123
"Win/Win Guidelines for Conflict Resolution 124
Activity: "Killer Statements Hurt" 125

VI. Focus on Apathetic Students 127

Helpful Hints for Dealing with "Apathetic Students" 128
Eight Ways to Increase Motivation in the Classroom 128
Practical Tips for Motivating Students 129
Motivation Systems Theory...131
Mystery Motivators 132
Principal's Round Table 135
"Unmotivated Students" 137
People Become Motivated When Their Basic Needs Are Met 140
Research on Strategies for Motivating Students 141
Underachievement Checklist 142
Ten Gifts for Children 144
Ways to Say, "Good for You!"...145
Famous People Who Survived "Difficult Times" 146
Activity: "Toilet Paper in the 'I Can'" 148
Activity: "Kick-Offs for Success" 149
Goal Setting Worksheet 150
Other Affirming Activities 151
"Daydreamers" 152
Activity: "Beat the Clock" 154
Activity: "One-Track Mind" 155
Activity: "Belonging" 156

VII. Trends in the Home 157

Abuse and Violence in the Home 158
Children and Television 160
Health Issues 162
Parenting in the '90's 165
Marriage and Divorce 169
Effects of Divorce on Children 172
What Are Educators Saying? 175
Education Over the Years 177

VIII. References 179

Books 181
Journals 182
Other Suggested Resources 182
Free Catalogs 188

About the Authors....................................190

The Nature of the "Difficult" Child

What is the first thing that comes to mind when you think of the term, "difficult student?" For most educators, it is a picture of a student who has been particularly challenging to work with. Mostly, the difficult student displays behaviors that interfere with their learning, or the learning of others. These students are more demanding of the teacher's time and energy than other students.

Difficult students are those who continue to provoke or evoke unpleasant feelings in others such as:

Frustration

Annoyance

Anger

Sadness

Concern

Hurt

Fear

In other words, a "difficult" child is one who is perceived as difficult to reach for some reason.

© 1998, YouthLight, Inc.

Things to Remember About Difficult Students

1. **Difficult Students Evoke Unpleasant Feelings in Others**

   Difficult students are those who evoke the following kinds of feelings in those who are working to help them:
Sadness	(disappointment to depression)
Fear	(uncertainty to terror)
Anger	(frustration to rage)

2. **A student who is difficult for one helper may not be difficult for another.**

   This occurs because the:
   - Child perceives one adult as more caring, accepting, understanding, trustworthy, and/or playful than the other.
   - Child unconsciously projects underlying anxiety to the adult and/or one or more other students in the classroom.
   - Adults have different tolerance levels for different kinds of student behavior.
   - Adult lacks critical information about the child or child's world.
   - Adult lacks the skills to reach the child.
   - Adult lacks the confidence to apply the strategies and skills needed for the child.
   - Adult has become personally invested and has lost professional objectivity or perspective in situation.

3. **Any student may be a "difficult student" at one time or another.**

4. **Some students become more difficult because they don't perceive themselves as valued by the helper(s).**

5. **It becomes much more challenging to think of a child as "difficult" once you know his or her underlying story - and every child has his or her story.**

6. **When developing an intervention plan for difficult students, remember:**

   - For persistently difficult students, educators should develop a team approach and not continue to "spin wheels" through the same efforts of one person.

   - Family members are important in the intervention process, but if they are not available, there are other people who might make a difference.

© 1998, YouthLight, Inc.

"High Risk"
vs.
"Difficult" Children

All "High Risk" students are not necessarily difficult. In fact, some high risk students are the opposite of "difficult." For example, the "teacher's pet" would not usually be considered by the teacher as a difficult student to work with. However, this student may be at risk socially and emotionally. Many of these students are "over pleasers" and are trying too hard to feel worthwhile through pleasing someone else.

On the other hand, not all difficult students are high risk. It is healthy and even expected that a child will test limits occasionally. The child becomes high risk when the intensity, frequency, and/or duration of these behaviors are significantly greater than usual for his or her age/grade level.

How then, should we define "difficult students?" Write some key terms below that you think should be included in a definition of this term.

Key Terms:

_____ _____

_____ _____

_____ _____

Difficult Students (a definition):

_____

_____

_____

_____

© 1998, YouthLight, Inc.

Underlying Causes of Difficult Behavior in Students

To understand a "difficult student" look at:

1. Psychological Needs (based on Glasser's "control theory")
    - Survival
    - Love/Belonging
    - Power
    - Freedom
    - Fun

2. Environmental Contexts
    - Family
    - Community
    - Culture
    - School and Classroom
    - Peers
    - Media

3. Personal Characteristics/Traits (Myrick & Bowman)
    - Physical
    - Social
    - Affective
    - Beliefs and Attitudes
    - Skills and Abilities

4. Your Own Responses
    - Communication Style (verbal and nonverbal)
    - Sensitivity
    - Objectivity

© 1998, YouthLight, Inc.

Managing the "Difficult Classroom"

Sometimes a teacher is confronted not with just a few difficult students, but with an entire class that is exceptionally difficult to manage. It is interesting that when the most difficult student is removed from the classroom for a significant length of time, another student sometimes takes over the role left vacant. This is because some classes develop into strong systems that function more as a group than as individual members.

A system is more than the sum of its parts (1+1=3). To understand and transform a difficult classroom requires looking at the students as a system that contains the following three elements:

1. Persecutors
2. Victims
3. Rescuers

Like a healthy family, the well functioning classroom system contains open communication between all members, clear roles and expectations, mutual respect, and reasonable limits.

© 1998, YouthLight, Inc.

The Difficult Classroom

Characteristics:

A difficult classroom may be:

- Overwhelming
- Crisis centered and primarily reactive
- Overly noisy
- Hostile
- Violent
- Disrespectful
- Ambivalent
- Chaotic
- Unfriendly
- Nonaccepting
- Unresponsive

Underlying Causes:

1. School System
   - Lack of heterogeneous grouping.
   - Disproportionate number of dysfunctioning students.
   - Lack of support personnel for the class.
   - Lack of emphasis on cooperative learning.
   - Lack of staff teamwork.
   - Physical environment of the classroom.
   - Overcrowded class.
   - Toxic grouping—class group does not gel for unforeseen reasons.
   - Teacher lacks:
     - A. Information
     - B. Skills
     - C. Confidence
     - D. Objectivity

2. Family and/or Community
   - Sociological and cultural issues
   - Family issues
   - Multilingual grouping
   - Unrest
   - Violence
   - Life style (e.g., substance abuse)
   - Impoverishness (inadequate medical, safety, nutrition, or emotional support)

© 1998, YouthLight, Inc.

3. Extraneous Circumstances
　　　-Time of year—stress and excitement around holidays and end of the school year.
　　　-Weather conditions.
　　　-Political & economic state of the country or region.

Strategies:

1. Involve parents and guardians.
   - Make lots of home visits and phone calls.
   - Send home lots of notes and letters.
   - Hold several parent-teacher meetings and be sure to separate the deeds from the doers and emphasize to parents positive qualities in their child.
   - Invite them to become involved in their school.
     - Active recruitment by PTO or PTA members
     - Mentors
     - Tutors
     - Storytellers
     - School helpers
     - Attendees in workshops and seminars held at school and/or in the community.

2. Start each year with a series of ice-breakers and team-builders which encourage students to build a cooperative momentum.

3. Set aside times for classroom meetings to discuss issues related to the class.

4. Establish the cooperation of the classroom in dealing with disruptive as well as positive behaviors.

5. Keep classroom rules to a minimum and word them in positive encouraging terms. Involve students in formulating the rules and consequences to build a sense of ownership.

6. Be consistent in enforcing rules and consequences, but not rigid. You can make occasional exceptions and still be fair because each child is different.

7. Provide the students with acceptable outlets for frustration or tension.

8. Watch what and how you command and confront the class. Many crises that occur in a classroom are triggered when a child feels backed into a corner and feels there can be no saving of grace.

9. When confronting, choose your words carefully. Use specific behavioral commands instead of judgmental statements. Provide consequences with a firm, but calm voice.

10. Agree with the students on a signal which will serve as a reminder when disruptive behavior begins.

11. When all else fails, try using appropriate humor.

12. Recognize times when the child or children are able to get along well in the classroom. Avoid saying that a child or classroom always behaves poorly. This may set up a failure identity or a self-fulfilling prophecy.

© 1998, YouthLight, Inc.

13. Avoid responding with anger or sarcasm. This tends to reinforce the idea that inappropriate behavior actually does get results.

14. Try to incorporate the negative experience into a positive learning experience for the classroom.

15. Assure to the child or class understand that it is their behavior, not them personally, that you are displeased with.

16. Help the child or class understand that they are responsible for their own actions.

17. Set up group incentives toward which the class can cooperatively work.

18. Provide choices for the child or class. Offer consequences as well as incentives which are motivating for that particular student or classroom.

19. The seating arrangement determines the patterns of communication within the classroom. Look at several alternative seating arrangements and change them as needed.

20. Use "time out" to isolate students, but allow them to return when they are ready to exhibit the desired behavior. Allow students to take "time out" on their own when they need it.

21. Use role-play, stories, puppets, or media to explore classroom cooperation.

22. Every staff member should have at least one person they can talk with at their school, openly and confidentially.

23. Find an ally. Each staff member should develop a collaborative relationship with another staff member.

24. Use the "Survival Skills for the Classroom Teacher."

© 1998, YouthLight, Inc.

Ten Ways to Quiet a Classroom

❶ Raise your hand in the air.

❷ Count to 3 or to a particular number.

❸ Have students raise one hand.

❹ Use the touchdown method.

❺ Ring a bell.

❻ Dim the lights.

❼ Be silent.

❽ Sing a song.

❾ Talk softly.

❿ Do something unusual.

© 1998, YouthLight, Inc.

Survival Skills for the Classroom Teacher

When all else has failed:

- Involve the class in a movement activity that regains teacher control.

- Use silence to help you regain composure and draw attention.

- Use a soft-spoken "broken record" approach.

- Use a time out for the entire classroom.

- Catch the students off-guard by doing something strangely unexpected.

- Call in your staff ally and swap classrooms for a while.

- Send a child, or small group of children, to your staff ally's room, not as a punitive act, but as a change of scene.

- Make sure you take care of yourself.

    - Have at least one major outside interest that is not directly related to your work as an educator.

    - Have one or more "significant others" to relate with outside of your work.

    - Exercise regularly, and watch your diet.

    - Keep learning new things and changing your routine. Don't allow yearly routine to build up boredom or complacency.

    - Keep playfulness in your teaching style.

    - Now and then, close your book and lesson plans, and teach spontaneously from your heart.

    - Take a mental health day before you really need it.

© 1998, YouthLight, Inc.

"Center Time"

PURPOSES:

To help the class learn to follow directions.
To help children learn cooperation.

PROCEDURE:

1. Depending on the number of children in your small group, set up an equal amount of "centers". For example, if you have 5 children, centers may be as follows:

    ❶ Reading
    ❷ Drawing
    ❸ Puzzles
    ❹ Blocks
    ❺ Football

    You may even block off a certain area for the child to stay in. You may use hula hoops, rope, or tape.

2. Explain to the children how each center will work, and the rotation order.

3. Using a timer, tell the children they are to do the activity until time is called. They are to move quickly into the next area.

4. If they become distracted from their task or do not move quickly, they are awarded one point. Three points will put them out of the game.

5. If the children are fairly good at doing this, you may want to try to distract them when each child has visited each center.

FOLLOW UP:

*   Have students discuss what they did to help them complete the tasks and ignore distractions.

*   Lead a discussion about cooperation, self-control and concentration, and how they were important factors in this task.

*   Have students explore ways they can use this during different times at school.

© 1998, YouthLight, Inc.

"Cooperation Game"

© 1998, YouthLight, Inc.

PURPOSES:

To demonstrate the value of cooperation in the classroom.

To help children develop listening skills.

To help children develop self-control

To teach children problem solving skills.

PROCEDURE:

1. One balloon will be needed.

2. Children are asked to sit on the floor (preferably Indian style).

3. The rules of the game are as follows:
   - Children cannot get up off their knees to hit the balloon.
   - If the balloon goes out of bounds or beyond the child's reach, the game is called.
   - Children are challenged to bat the balloon in the air 100 times.
   - Children are told that either everyone will win or everyone will lose.

4. Each time the balloon goes out of bounds or a child gets off his knees and the game is called, discussion proceeds as follows:
   - What is the problem?
   - How can we solve the problem?
   - Let's implement the solution.

FOLLOW-UP:

Should the children achieve their goals, discuss:
- How did we accomplish our goal? Cooperation, listening, following directions, working together.
- When we had problems, what did we do?
- How could we all work together in the classroom?
- Everyone do their part in listening carefully and cooperating.

Should the children achieve their goals, discuss:
- What happened so that we did not accomplish our goals?
- What did we do right?
- What could we do differently next time?

12

"Connecting*"

PURPOSE:

To encourage children to build friendships with others in the classroom.

PROCEDURE:

1. Divide the class into groups of four people.

2. One person is asked to lie down on a large sheet of paper.

3. Draw an outline around the student's body.

4. The group then lists on each of the body parts things that they have in common. For example:

> **Head** - things we like to think about
> **Eyes** - things we like to see
> **Ears** - things we like to hear/listen to
> **Mouth** - things we like to talk about
> **Stomach** - things we like to eat
> **Heart** - things we feel strongly about
> **Hands** - things we like to make
> **Shoulders** - problems we have
> **Feet** - places we've gone and would like to go

5. These pictures can be shared with the larger group.

FOLLOW UP:

- Encourage each group to discuss why it is important to talk about how people are similar to each other.

- Have the class discuss the importance of accepting the things that are different between people.

© 1998, YouthLight, Inc.

* From: Foster, E., Energizers and Icebreakers

Encouraging Student Involvement

Encourage contributions of student to class.

Allow students to be helpers.

Give students choices in environment.

Ask for students' input for rules.

Allow students the opportunity to say positive things to each other.

© 1998, YouthLight, Inc.

Thirty-One Incentive Plans

1. Have a jar for marbles. Each time the class is doing a good job, move a marble into the jar. When there are x amount of marbles or the marbles reach a certain level, the class would be entitled to a particular award such as a popcorn party, movie, etc.

2. Teresa Painter, a teacher in Monroe, North Carolina was studying Indians. During this study unit, she allowed children to earn a feather for their headdress for each positive thing she caught them doing in the classroom. At the end of a predetermined time, the children wore their headdresses in a parade. Needless to say, some "Indians" had very long headdresses while others did not have as many.

3. Roberta Collins, a teacher in Monroe, North Carolina uses a car system. (Good for younger children). Each child's name is written on a car. A big spotlight is placed in a central location in the room. All students' cars are placed on the green light at the beginning of the day. If a rule is broken, the child's car is moved to yellow. If another rule is broken, the car is moved to red. Each move of the car would carry a consequence for the child. At the end of he week, any child who's car had not been moved is given a reward.

4. Other teachers use the bee system. Each child's name is placed on a bee. As long as the child has good behavior, the child is able to stay in the bee hive. As children are good throughout the day, the bee can be moved in increments to the honey jar. The teacher might have a prize jar entitled the "honey jar." Rules might even use the "be" word frequently. For example, "Be a good listener." "Be respectful of other people's property." "Be a good friend by not fighting."

5. Benton Heights Elementary has used an entire school incentive system by using a train theme. Rules for the school are listed on trains and students are awarded "Staying on Track" coupons for good behavior. The rules for this program include the following:
   - One point will be awarded for each student caught being good.
   - Entire classrooms will be awarded 10 points or entire class good behavior.
   - A teacher cannot give his or her class coupons.
   - A teacher can give coupons to any other student or any other classroom.
   - Coupons can be given by special teachers, regular teachers, principals, and any other school personnel.
   - Classes compete to determine which one can accumulate the most points on a monthly basis.
   - This class is given a winner's banner to hang outside the classroom and a party of some kind.

6. Some classes use the "stick" system. Each student has a pocket. As children break rules, a stick is placed in their pocket. Each stick would symbolize a consequence.

© 1998, YouthLight, Inc.

7. Fifth grades at Benton Heights use a chart for good behavior. The chart is broken down into the 5 letter grades of A, B, C, D, and F. Each letter grade has about 10 spaces per division. Children's names are placed on the chart. When rules are broken or homework is not completed, a check is placed on one of the spaces. At the end of nine weeks, each student who has kept their checks confined to the "A" division are able to go skating. Other students stay at school.

8. In order to determine rewards, one teacher puts various rewards inside of several balloons. When the class is eligible for a reward, the class chooses the balloon they would like to pop and pop it to see what they win. This creates a little element of surprise.

9. One teacher uses a football field to measure success. This teacher places a person at one end of the field. The teacher then offers incentives and rewards for possible movement of the person down the field. For example, if the class cleans up within 3 minutes, the person can move 2 yardage markers. If the class listens during the lecture, the person can be moved 3 yardage points. (Yardage points can vary from class to class.) Various class infractions may be worth penalty points in which the person would be moved back several yardage points. A touchdown might equal a reward of some kind. The teacher might keep a record of points accumulated during the week for a grand prize at the end of the week. For instance, if the class achieved 35 points, they could go outside for an extra 30 minutes. Other rewards could be used as well.

10. For students who keep their names off the board, do all their homework, and follow the rules, extra time could be awarded to them on Friday. 4th graders at Benton Heights call it Fantastic Friday. These students are able to play for an hour on Friday afternoon. Other students have to stay inside.

11. Other rewards might include "raise a grade" coupons, raffle tickets, movie parties, and VIP certificates.

12. A research study entitled "Grandma's Rule" was done by Cowen, Jones, and Bellack. These authors described a teacher doing a reading group with the goal being to get the rest of the class to do their seat work. The teacher stated that the children must work 15 minutes in order to get 15 minutes of free time. The teacher would use a stop watch. As long as the children were working, the clock continued. However, whenever anyone got out of their seat, started talking, got off-task, etc., the clock would stop until all had gotten back to task. Only 30 minutes or so were available. Therefore, when the clock stopped, children lost free time. Whenever the 15 minutes was completed, the children could have the remaining time in free time. Free time may consist of 5 minutes or 1 minute. The choice always rested with the children.

With such an approach, out of seat behavior decreased 42%, talking decreased 65%, and off task behavior decreased 66%. Authors cited free time, group contingency, and peer pressure as key ingredients for change.

© 1998, YouthLight, Inc.

13. Some teachers placed a strip of paper on a child's desk. Whenever the child is paying attention, a timer could be set to go off at variable intervals. Whenever the timer went off, students who were seated and doing their work would receive a check on the strip of paper. Different numbers of checks could be turned in for various privileges or rewards.

14. Hegerle, Kesecker, and Counch (1979) designed a game to reduce out of seat and talking out behaviors. Two class teams were formed and both teams were told they could win by receiving less than a pre-specified number of bad behavior points. For instance, every time a team misbehaves, they would receive a point. The teams with the least number of points won. Teams that won could get reinforcers such as play time, being first in line, etc. After two weeks, teams were required to have under 10 points to be the winners.

    Utilizing this method, disruptive behavior decreased immediately after the game began from almost 100% to between 8 and 15%.

    Note: Although the authors did not mention this, it would appear that this game could also be designed so that teams could earn positive points for positive behavior.

    If one child is having either academic or behavioral problems and the class is on a marble or chip system, this child can be told that they can earn the class a marble or chip for successful completion of academic or behavioral goals. This child is usually not very popular with peers and when given a chance to earn the classroom a reward, the class is encouraged to help and praise this child. The child usually likes this attention they receive and does well on this system.

15. Simmons and Wasik suggested putting target children in groups. The groups were asked to help the child complete the work. If the target child did the work, the group received 30 minutes free time at the end of the day. If the target child did not complete the work, the group did not receive free time. The authors used the seating arrangements, peer influence, and free time as motivators.

    Authors noted that students usually responded to requests to help peers more than to pay attention. Target children were more popular and authors noted more cooperation and independent work. This method was particularly effective with low achieving students. Authors cited teacher approval, free time, and peer helping to be the primary influencing factors of success for this method.

16. Daudargas, Madsen, and Scott designed a variable rate report for children to take home to parents. Children were told that at least one time per week they would be required to take a report home for parent signatures. To get a good report, assignment completion was required. This was defined as students needing to have 85% accuracy. Seven to nine students got reports daily.

    The study looked at fixed rates versus variable. The variable rates showed a marked increase in assignments completed. In fact, the rate of completed assignments increased 154%.

© 1998, YouthLight, Inc.

17. DeVries and Clavin did research on using a classroom reward system. The research had three components:
    - The class is divided into 4 or 5 teams of equal overall achievement levels. Team members drill newly learned material to each other to practice for tournaments.
    - These teams compete for points in tournaments. Points are accumulated weekly and findings can be published in the school newsletter.
    - Games are played to test skills and subject matter.

    Research was conducted with 3000 students and many positive results were noted. These included increased student liking, more cross-racial friendships, and more positive attitudes toward academic achievements.

18. Students are told that they will be working on a particular behavior such as listening, being respectful, being honest, etc. Prior to this, the teacher has written the names of each student and placed them in a bowl. At various times, the teacher can draw a name and if this student has been successful in the particular "behavior of the day," this student or the whole class can win a reward.

19. One teacher placed a rabbit in her room and let the rabbit be free while the children were in class. She reported that the animal kept the students from running around the room and had a calming effect. For those that seemed to have emotional problems, it provided an outlet. One little boy whispered to the bunny and loved to pet the bunny. Therefore, the rabbit also seemed to have a therapeutic effect.

20. The teacher could write a word on the board like "On task" or "Homework." Underneath each letter, the teacher draws 25 or 30 blocks. Each time a student is caught doing this particular behavior, the student is told they can put their name in a block. Whenever the blocks are filled up, the teacher can choose a letter and number and call it out. For instance, if the word was on task, the teacher might call T-15 and this student would win the prize.

21. Provide student with an AB card which can be used for discounts in the community.

22. One school in a small community has a Parade of Excellence in which students who have good grades and good behavior all march together in a parade through the downtown.

23. Three consequences have been described by author Lee Swanson and are as follows:
    - For every noise talk-out, the student was charged with 2 minutes from his lunch period. During this time the student had to attend tutoring sessions with the teacher. Talk-outs decreased from 18 per 30 minutes to 4. They continued at a rate of 8-1/2.
    - For inappropriate behavior for another student a token system was established that gave the students ten tokens before a particular academic assignments. Each time the student talked out, a token was taken away. Remaining tokens could purchase time for desired behaviors. Disruptive behavior declined to 1/6 of its original level.
    - Four students who were acting out with each other were given 20 tokens. If any one of the students disturbed anyone in class, each student lost a token. Tokens retained by students at the end of the day could be used to purchase time doing various enjoyable activ-

© 1998, YouthLight, Inc.

ities. During this treatment, disturbing others and leaving seats decreased by half and talk outs by 2/3, and cursing by more than 80%.

24. Authors Azrin and Powers describe a positive practice of improving conduct in particular, talking out and leaving assigned seats. Children are taught the rules of the classroom for several days. If a child breaks a rule, they would be required to practice the rule in class and then stay in from recess and practice the behavior for 5 to 10 minutes. After the practice session, the student could return to recess.

    During various aspects of this study when warnings and reminders alone were given, disruptions remained high - an average on 29 per day. Just the loss of recess reduced them by 60%. However, delayed and immediate positive practice lowered inappropriate behavior by 95 and 98%.

25. One teacher has students repeat the behavior they are about to perform several times before they do it. For instance the teacher might have students repeat, "We are going to do a great job in the cafeteria." She reports that this method seems to help her children obtain a predetermined attitude of success.

26. Ellery and Black used a token economy system in which students were rewarded with a token for each 5 minutes of appropriate behavior. Students were told they would receive a reward once they reached 5 tokens. However, no child could receive a reward unless all children have 5 tokens.

27. In order to decrease inappropriate remarks by one student, authors Lovitt, Lovitt, Eaton, and Kirkwood designed a program in which the disruptive student's good friend was employed to help the teacher. The good friend was instructed to help the disruptive friend by doing the following:
    • Each time the disruptive student said an inappropriate remark, the friend was to tell him that he did not like it when he said
    • The friend was then to move away from the disruptive student.
    • The disruptive student could then be prompted by the teacher to make appropriate statements. If the student complied with the teacher, the friend could come back.
    With this approach and after used 60 times, the level was maintained during the following school year.

28. Use a predetermined plan to be completed with students after misbehaving. The form would have a section for problem to continue, and a plan for correcting the problem. Teacher and student could come to an agreement.

29. Some schools have time out rooms (different form in school suspension rooms) in which students can go and calm down during disruptive times. The students have a choice in the room - talk to the person monitoring the room and make a plan or cool off themselves and return to the room. This method hopefully gives students a chance to regain composure on their own and is not seen as a punitive measure.

© 1998, YouthLight, Inc.

30. In dealing with students who have difficulty coming in from a "fun" activity or a special class and getting ready again for academic learning, Struble suggests the following intervention. The teacher was to tell the class members that they would be timed on how long they took to get ready for work. Immediate praise was given to students who demonstrated quick readiness. The teacher then monitored progress and eventually the time to get ready for class stabilized at one minute. Again, the teacher used reinforcement and the class monitored their own progress.

31. Note: This method may be more suitable for a self-contained class.

The numbers 1-25 were listed in decreasing order on the board. As an infraction was committed, the highest number was marked off with the offending child's name placed beside the number that was crossed off. At the end of an hour, all students were given the highest number still left on the board in tokens.

Individual contingencies could also be used by placing an individual's name on the board with the numbers and crossing off numbers as infractions are committed.

In both the individual and group contingency methods, disruptive behaviors decreased by 88% in one classroom and 94% in another.

REFERENCES:

Axelrod, S. (1973) Comparison of individual and group contingencies in two special classes. Behavior Therapy, 4, 83-90.

Azrin, N.H., and Powers, M.A. (1975) Eliminating classroom disturbances of emotionally disturbed children by positive practice procedures. Behavior Therapy, 6, 525-534.

Cowen, R.J., Jones, F.H., and Bellack, A.S. (1979) Grandma's rule with group contingencies - A cost efficient means of classroom management. Behavior Modification, 3, 397-418.

Daudargas, R.W., Madsen, C.H., Jr., and Scott, J.W. (1977) Differential effects of fixed and variable time feedback on production rates of elementary school children. Journal of Applied Behavior Analysis, 10, 673-678.

DeVries, D.L., and Slavin, R.E. (1978) Teams-Games-Tournaments (TGT): Review of ten classroom experiments." Journal of Research and Development in Education, 12 28-38.

Ellery, M.D., and Black, W.A.M. (1975) Reduction of disruptive behavior in the classroom: group and individual reinforcement contingencies compared. New Zealand Journal of Educational Studies, 10, 59-65.

Hegerle, D.R. Kesecker, M.P., and Couch, J.V. (1979) A Behavior Game for the Reduction of Inappropriate Classroom Behaviors. School Psychology Digest, 8, 339-343.

© 1998, YouthLight, Inc.

Lovitt, T.C., Lovitt, A.D., Eaton, M.D. and Kirkwood, M. (1973)The declaration of inappropriate comments by a natural consequence. Journal of School Psychology, 11, 148-154.

Simmons, J.T., and Wasik, B.H. (1976) Grouping strategies, peer influence, and free time as classroom management techniques with first and third grade children. Journal of School Psychology,14, 322-332.

Struble, J.B. (1971)The application of positive social reinforcement of the behaviors of getting ready to work. School Applications of Learning Theory, 1, 34-39.

Swanson, L. (1979) Removal of Positive Reinforcement to Alter Learning Disabled Adolescent's Preacademic Problems. Psychology in the Schools, 16, 286-292.

© 1998, YouthLight, Inc.

Tips for Surviving a "Difficult Classroom"

1. Learn how to say "No." Practice saying it without reservation, without hesitation, in an "I-mean-it" tone of voice.

2. Prioritize your activities so that you can space them out more efficiently.

3. Remember that, "The only way to have a friend is to be one." (Emerson)

Problem-Solving Steps for Children

Gather Data
1. Get information from both children.

2. Ask questions calmly and acceptingly.

3. Ask feeling questions to help children learn empathy.

Define the Problem

Generate Alternatives
1. Encourage brainstorming.

2. Help children come up with ideas rather than adults doing it for them. (This will help children learn to process more effectively.)

3. Do not evaluate as you go. This may stifle creativity.

4. Evaluate each alternative.
   - Look at each idea to determine consequences.

   - Help children evaluate the ideas.

5. Determine a solution.
   - Encourage solutions in which everyone wins if possible.

6. Implement the solution.

© 1998, YouthLight, Inc.

Using Negotiation in Child-Teacher Conflicts

1. **Stop**

2. **Identify the problem**

3. **Generate ideas**

4. **Evaluate ideas**

5. **Develop a plan**

Special Concerns:

1. Hunt for win-win situations that will work for teachers and students.

2. Let children know their feelings are important.

3. Allow children to come up with ideas.

4. Write down all ideas.

5. Involve everyone affected by the decision.

6. Help children understand the concept of choices as it applies to self-control.

7. Describe the behavior instead of evaluating it.

8. Be firm but friendly.

9. Control negative emotions.

10. Avoid escalating the situation.

11. Allow students to save face.

© 1998, YouthLight, Inc.

Interventions When the Student's Need Is Power *

1. When teachers acknowledge that they can't dominate, they can gain cooperation from students rather than confrontation.

2. Acknowledge the student's power. When we give up our power and control, the student has nothing to resist. People who feel dominated often react by resisting the person in charge.

3. Realize that teachers cannot "make" students do things. Realize that we can threaten, take away rights and privileges, and send notes home, but until the student chooses to do the work, it will not get done.

4. Remove the audience so that the student will not be reinforced by the crowd. Conflicts may intensify when others are watching to see who will win. More seems to be at stake.

5. Name the student's behavior and inform the student that you would be willing to talk or to discuss the matter in a calm voice. If this is not possible at the time of the conflict, make an appointment to do this later.

6. Use a "fogging" technique. Act as if the negative statements are of little or no value to you. Basically you are saying that you will not allow the student to manipulate you. Active listening will only prolong the confrontation.

7. Agree with the student as much as possible. This way the student has less to disagree with. (e.g. If a student says you're a horrible teacher, respond, "You may be right, now do problem #4.")

8. Use time-out in the school. The teacher may want to give choices, i.e. time-out in present room or in another teacher's room. (e.g. "Would you like to go alone or with another adult?")

9. Time-outs should be increased if behavior continues.

10. Use "when-then" statements. When you do this behavior, then _____ will happen.

11. Establish clear consequences. Appropriate consequences are:
    *   Related to the misbehavior. (e.g. "If you tip the chair, you will stand for the rest of the period.)
    *   Reasonable. (e.g. If the child scribbled on the door, reasonable consequences would be to scrub the door. But, to scrub every door in the building would be unreasonable.)

© 1998, YouthLight, Inc.

Interventions When the Student's Need Is Power *

1. When teachers acknowledge that they can't dominate, they can gain cooperation from students rather than confrontation.

2. Acknowledge the student's power. When we give up our power and control, the student has nothing to resist. People who feel dominated often react by resisting the person in charge.

3. Realize that teachers cannot "make" students do things. Realize that we can threaten, take away rights and privileges, and send notes home, but until the student chooses to do the work, it will not get done.

4. Remove the audience so that the student will not be reinforced by the crowd. Conflicts may intensify when others are watching to see who will win. More seems to be at stake.

5. Name the student's behavior and inform the student that you would be willing to talk or to discuss the matter in a calm voice. If this is not possible at the time of the conflict, make an appointment to do this later.

6. Use a "fogging" technique. Act as if the negative statements are of little or no value to you. Basically you are saying that you will not allow the student to manipulate you. Active listening will only prolong the confrontation.

7. Agree with the student as much as possible. This way the student has less to disagree with. (e.g. If a student says you're a horrible teacher, respond, "You may be right, now do problem #4.")

8. Use time-out in the school. The teacher may want to give choices, i.e. time-out in present room or in another teacher's room. (e.g. "Would you like to go alone or with another adult?")

9. Time-outs should be increased if behavior continues.

10. Use "when-then" statements. When you do this behavior, then _____ will happen.

11. Establish clear consequences. Appropriate consequences are:
    - Related to the misbehavior. (e.g. "If you tip the chair, you will stand for the rest of the period.)
    - Reasonable. (e.g. If the child scribbled on the door, reasonable consequences would be to scrub the door. But, to scrub every door in the building would be unreasonable.)

- Respectful and conscious of student's self-esteem.
12. Know the difference between consequences and punishment. Consequences reflect the above. Punishments are not related, reasonable, or respectful. Punishment provokes hostility and antagonism.

13. Jane Nelson describes the following results when using punishments instead of consequences.
   - Resentment: "This is unfair - I don't trust adults."
   - Revenge: "They're winning, I'll get even."
   - Retreat: "I'm getting away."
   - Rebellion: " I won't get caught next time."
   - Reduced self-esteem: "I'm a bad person."

© 1998, YouthLight, Inc.

* From: Alpert, L. <u>Cooperative Discipline</u>

Improving Students' Social Skills

(Good for a small group)

---

1. Find an appropriate task for children to complete as a group, e.g. building blocks, a large puzzle, etc.

2. Determine a social skill to work on in this session, e.g. sharing, taking turns, saying please, practicing good manners. Explain what these social skills "look and sound" like.

3. Children are told that they will have an allotted amount of time to work on this task. Each time you notice an appropriate social skill, the child is to be rewarded with a chip, ticket or token.

4. At the end of the time period children are asked to "self evaluate." In other words, children are asked to share with the group the reasons they feel they were awarded tokens.

5. Other processing can include how they can use these social skills in the classroom.

© 1998, YouthLight, Inc.

Crisis Management
How To Help Those You Care About

1. Understand that emotional consequences follow a traumatic experience.

2. Don't expect that the person you care about will "get better" in a certain amount of time or in a certain way. Often recovery is a long and difficult process. If the person requires more time than you expected, you may feel frustrated or even angry.

3. Tell the survivor how you feel: that you are sorry they have been hurt.

4. Encourage the survivor to talk to you about how they feel. When they do, listen without interrupting or making judgements about what you hear. All the survivors feelings are okay even if you might not feel the same way.

5. Remind the survivor that their confusing emotions are normal.

6. Do not attempt to impose your explanation on why this has happened to the survivor. It probably won't be the explanation the survivor believes and imposing yours might hurt your relationship with them.

7. Do not tell the survivor, "I know how you feel" or "Everything will be all right." Often, these statements are really efforts to relieve your own anxiety about how you feel about what has happened to the survivor. Survivors say that when they hear these statements, they think that people do not care about or understand them.

8. Go to any court hearings, community meetings, or other appointments that relate to the trauma. This is an important way to provide support to the survivor.

9. Be willing to say nothing. Just being there is often all that you can do to help.

10. Don't be afraid to encourage a survivor to ask for help in the form of a post-trauma counseling. You might even go to the first appointment to show your support and concern.

© 1998, YouthLight, Inc.

The Process of Crisis Intervention

1. **Make contact at a feeling level.**

    - Identify student's feeling via active listening.
    - Accept student's right to feel in this manner.
    - Use statements rather than questions.

2. **Explore the problem now.**

    - Identify precipitating events.
    - Focus on immediate events.
    - Come to a joint understanding and description of the problem as it is now.

3. **Summarize the problem with the student so that you both agree on a definition of the problem's main elements.**

4. **Focus on the problem.**

    - Agree with the student on those areas where joint energies should be spent at this time.
    - Areas selected should be of most concern.
    - Areas selected should be susceptible to some immediate action with likelihood of results.

5. **Explore resources.**

    - Motivate and direct the student to tell you about what actions might be taken.
    - What would the student like to do, what is she afraid to do, who can be used as support, etc.
    - After student has explored resources, you can make suggestions.

6. **Contract**

    - Agree on plan of action with student.
    - Specify next step, what she will do, what you will do.
    - Specify goals,
    - Have clear methods for follow-up, emergencies, if necessary.

© 1998, YouthLight, Inc.

Immediate Post-Trauma Debriefing

Post-trauma debriefings are most effective when they occur two to five days after the incident.

Debriefings should be mandatory for all persons involved in the critical incident and follow this format:

1. Setting the stage

2. To begin the debriefings, any necessary introductions are made. The ground rules, including confidentiality, are discussed and the agenda presented.

3. Looking at the Consequences of Survival

    Each debriefing participant describes their post-trauma situation - what their life is like at this time.

4. Understanding the Consequences of Survival

    Information concerning Critical Incident Stress is presented, including the normal results of the exposure to critical incidents and expectations for recovery.

5. Contracting for Recovery

    Each participant develops a plan for recovery that will assist in the management of Critical Incident Stress and reduce the possibility of long-term post-trauma stress.

6. Closing and Evaluating

    The debriefings include a follow-up session three to four weeks after the initial session.

© 1998, YouthLight, Inc.

Parent Coupon Booklet

One of the most frustrating aspects of working with difficult students is the lack of parental support. Quite often difficult students come from single-parent homes or low-income homes. These parents have a hard time getting to school during the day to see a teacher or participate in school activities because they are unable to get away from their jobs for a period of time. These parents often have low paying jobs and they cannot afford to lose two or three hours of work to come to school . . . this loss of hours may mean less money for food, gas, etc. The Parent Coupon Booklet is a practical idea that allows parents to leave work for a short period of time without losing pay.

The Parent Coupon Booklet Program

1. At the start of the school year, the PTO or PTA provides every parent at the school with a Parent Coupon Booklet. The booklet contains ten coupons. Each coupon is worth one hour off from work without loss of pay.

2. The school notifies local businesses, factories, industries and other employers in the area about this program. A letter encourages the employers to "support education" and allow employees to redeem the coupons so their workers can attend school during the day without loss of pay.

3. At the end of the school year, each employer who accepted the coupons are invited to attend a luncheon at the school to show the school's appreciation for their support. Business owners or managers are invited and they receive an attractive certificate from the school.

4. Also, throughout the school year, the local newspaper listed and thanked businesses for their support. Businesses like to see their names listed in the newspaper as supporters of education.

5. Some schools also add other coupons to the booklet. These "extra" coupons are for discounts and "freebies" from local businesses.

6. Another idea for this program is to place "redeemed" coupons in a box and have monthly drawings for prizes for parents who attended school thanks to the program.

7. Schools may wish to plan other activities around this program. The program has great potential to increase involvement and it gives businesses an avenue to show their support.

© 1998, YouthLight, Inc.

"Attention Seekers"

"Gossipers/Tattlers," & "Class Clowns"

"Attention Seekers" are students who are attempting to meet their need for attention. Many attention seekers are attempting to meet their needs for love and belonging, and, to a somewhat lesser extent, for power and/or fun.

© 1998, YouthLight, Inc.

Helpful Hints for Dealing with "Attention Seekers"

1. Do a flip-flop. That is, turn an attention-getting device into a learning experience.

2. Ignore whatever the child is doing.

3. Praise the child for something that has nothing whatever to do with his bid for attention.

4. Talk to the child privately about his or her ways of asking for attention. It may not have occurred to the student that that was what he/she was doing. Between the two of you, devise a check plan that will help him or her realize the extent of the attention-getting behavior.

© 1998, YouthLight, Inc.

ADD/ADHD
Attention Deficit Hyperactivity Disorder (ADHD)

According to the criteria in the Diagnostic and Statistical Manual of the American Psychiatric Association, to diagnose a child as having ADHD, he/she must display for six months or more, at least eight of the following characteristics before the age of seven.

1. Fidgets, squirms or seems restless
2. Has difficulty remaining seated
3. Is easily distracted
4. Has difficulty awaiting turn
5. Blurts out something
6. Has difficulty following instructions
7. Has difficulty sustaining attention
8. Shifts from one incompleted task to another
9. Has difficulty playing quietly
10. Talks excessively
11. Interrupts or intrudes on others
12. Does not seem to listen
13. Often loses things necessary for tasks
14. Frequently engages in dangerous actions

Undifferentiated Attention Deficit Disorder

In this form of ADD, the primary and most significant characteristic is inattentiveness; hyperactivity is not present. Nevertheless, these children still manifest problems with organization and distractibility and they may be seen as quiet or passive in nature. It is speculated that Undifferentiated ADD is currently underdiagnosed as these children tend to be overlooked more easily in the classroom. Thus these children may be at a higher risk for academic failure than those with attention deficit hyperactivity disorder.

© 1998, YouthLight, Inc.

Teaching Students with Attention Deficit Disorders

In his book, <u>The ADD Hyperactivity Handbook for Schools</u>, Harvey C. Parker suggests some of the following:

1. Seat ADD students near teacher's desk, but include as part of regular class seating.

2. Surround ADD students with "good role models."

3. Place ADD students up front with his or her back to the rest of the class to keep other students out of view.

4. Avoid distractions such as noisy air conditioner, heater, doors, windows, and high traffic areas.

5. Remember that ADD children to not handle change well, so avoid such things as changed in schedule, transitions, disruptions.

6. Be creative. Produce a "stimuli-reduced study area."

Recommendations for Students Performing Assignments

1. Give out only one assignment at a time.

2. Monitor frequently.

3. Modify assignments as needed. Develop an individualized educational program.

4. Make sure you are testing knowledge and not attention span.

5. Give extra time for certain tasks. The ADD student may work slowly. Do not penalize for needed extra time.

6. ADD children are easily frustrated. Stress, fatigue, and pressure can break down the ADD child's self-control and lead to poor behavior.

© 1998, YouthLight, Inc.

Recommendations for Behavior Modification and Self-Esteem Enhancement

1. Remain calm, state infraction of rule, and don't debate or argue.

2. Have pre-established consequences for misbehavior.

3. Administer consequences immediately and monitor behavior frequently.

4. Enforce rules of the classroom consistently.

5. Discipline should be appropriate to "fit the crime," without harshness.

6. Avoid ridicule and criticism.

7. Avoid publicly reminding students on medication to "take their medication."

Providing Encouragement

1. Reward more than you punish.

2. Praise immediately any and all good behavior and performance.

3. Change rewards if not effective in motivating behavioral change.

4. Find ways to encourage the child.

5. Teach the child to reward him or herself

6. Help students to use a daily assignment notebook to keep up with work.

© 1998, YouthLight, Inc.

Gossipers/Tattlers

Characteristics:

1. They may tell "stories" about others to peers (gossip) or adults (tattling).
2. Their stories may involve legitimate concerns, or be manipulative.

Underlying Causes:

1. They may have legitimate concerns about their safety and may need adult protection.
2. They may feel the need to "elevate" their value as seen by others.
3. They may exhibit these behaviors as a means of getting attention from others.
4. They may not have the ability to solve, or cope with problems in other ways.
5. Their parents may have solved many of their child's battles and thereby deprived the child of opportunities to learn problem solving concepts, skills, and confidence.
6. They may want to have fun and/or feel powerful by initiating conflict between others.
7. They may be striking out or seeking revenge at someone due to feelings such as hurt, anger, and jealousy.

Strategies:

1. Teach children acceptable reasons for gossiping or tattling, i.e., safety concerns or someone being hurt.
2. Avoid talking negatively about students yourself, in front of students or other educators.
3. Use cooperative learning.
4. Emphasize strength-building and affirmation activities in the classroom.
5. Don't overreact. Sometimes a lesser response will reduce the reinforcement of this behavior.
6. Teach children social skills for dealing with teasing, name-calling, aggressive attempts, etc.
7. Encourage independent behavior by rewarding pro-social skills.
8. Reward affirmations made by children in the class.
9. Use strategic humor to stop the gossip or tattling.
10. Teach "Refusal Skills" to help students refuse to be a link in the gossip chain.
11. Use "Share" (see next page).

© 1998, YouthLight, Inc.

Helpful Hints for Dealing
with "Gossipers"

1. Ask the gossiper if he/she is willing to put into writing the juicy morsel they just peddled to you.

2. Expect students to be positive, instead of negative, in their comments about others. Hopefully, the attitude generated in the regular classes will spill over into the students' purely social contacts.

3. Help students, through class discussions, learn how to cope with gossip when they are the ones gossiped about. They will be able to add to these suggestions: ignore the gossip; refrain from counter-charging; talk to someone you can trust; don't talk to everyone.

4. Resist the temptation to get "in on" the gossip that you sense is going around. Promptly discount 90% of what you overhear and put the other 10% into mental cold storage, just in case it proves significant later on. Knowing what you do, you may, in an ensuing discussion, diplomatically avert embarrassing situations.

Helpful Hints for Dealing
with "Tattlers"

1. Become aware of the student's social status with his peers and when possible, redirect antagonistic behavior. If, for instance, the tattler is on the same team with someone who dislikes him, make a change.

2. Interpret for the tattler what his behavior has done. The consequence of this behavior may impress him. ("Tim, while you used your time to tattle on May, your bus left.")

3. Join a minus with a plus. ("Susie, I didn't like to hear your tale about the boys, but I did like the way you said, "Excuse me" when you passed in front of Mr. Doe.")

4. Keep a mental record of the tattler's tales and when appropriate, praise him or her for tattling less and less.

5. Remind the student that tattling is unacceptable behavior in school and that it is different from reporting. ("Susie, see if you can tell me which of these statements is tattling and which is reporting: James pulled Jan's braids'; 'Mrs. Brand said to tell you the bus is here.'")

© 1998, YouthLight, Inc.

Strategies for Dealing with Tattling

Following is a list of specific activities to deal with tattling in the classroom.

1. **"My Concerns" Box**

    The teacher could make a "My Concerns" box. Students would be encouraged to write and then place any concerns or "tattles" they have in this box. (Note: This requires effort and will immediately cut down on some concerns.) At the end of the week, the teacher would take the box, turn it upside down and begin discussing concerns which have been written on the paper. This would in effect cause Monday's concerns to be on top and Friday's concerns to be on the bottom. Hopefully, some students will have forgotten some of the concerns. For example, the teacher might say, "Susan, it looks like you had a concern from Monday. Do you remember what that was?" If Susan says "No," the teacher might respond, "Well, that must mean that situation was taken care of. We'll just throw away that concern showing you aren't worried about that any longer." If Susan says "Yes," then the teacher might take a few minutes to discuss the situation and to allow the students to brainstorm appropriate solutions to the problems.

    This procedure should not take any more than 20 to 30 minutes of time. It can be used in conjunction with the class meeting. See below for details.

2. **"Pretzels"**

    Ruth Sidney Charney in <u>Teaching Children to Care</u> (1991) describes a wonderful idea called "Pretzels" designed to create, model and reinforce effective communication. It also provides a means by which children can provide a symbolic means of restitution for children when they use put downs. The goal of the activity is merely to provide some means of restitution to victims as well as to empower students to confront situations in a positive means.

    To implement this idea, the class would meet together one time per week. At this time, the teacher would give each student 10 pretzels. Students would then take turns saying one positive statement and one negative statement about the other children in the classroom. When the student says a positive statement about someone, they are asked to give that student one pretzel as a token of appreciation. When the student says a negative statement, the offending student is asked to give the reporting student one of their pretzels as a token of apology.

    Before the activity begins, the teacher must set certain guidelines. This is important especially during the reporting of negative acts. First, if one student says that another hurt him or her, the offending student is not allowed to argue as to whether or not he/she actually did the behavior in question. The teacher might explain this guideline by saying that we often

© 1998, YouthLight, Inc.

do not realize that we have hurt someone or may not have intended to hurt them by our actions. However, if a friend does become offended by our actions, it is important to say we are sorry in order to prevent friendships from being hurt or destroyed. Therefore, the pretzel must be given to show we are sorry.

As an extension of this activity, assign different negative actions to different costs depending on their intensity. For example, teasing may be worth two pretzels, hitting four pretzels, etc. These values may be decided by the teacher and class. Also, pretzels may be replaced with nuts, raisins, or other treats. "Pretzels" teaches children to communicate effectively with each other and deal with problems in an assertive manner. Hopefully, this will reduce tattling while equipping students with important life skills.

Charney, Ruth. (1991) Teaching Children to Care. Northeast Foundation for Children.

3. Class Meetings

Jane Nelson in Positive Discipline and William Glasser in Schools Without Failure suggests having "class meetings" to discuss problems students are having. To have an effective class meeting, both authors suggest having ground rules. Ground rules may include the following:

- No blaming or accusing other people.
- No punishing the class for the misbehavior of a few.
- No verbal or physical put downs.
- No interruptions.
- Listen to other people when they talk.
- Be solution oriented and work to come up with mutually agreed upon interventions for problems.

The teacher would then teach problem-solving techniques and allow the students to come up with solutions. This not only empowers students in the classroom, it makes them more responsible for their behaviors. In effect, this can reduce tattling by teaching students alternative ways to independently handle problems.

4. "I Can Handle It"

The teacher could make two envelopes or boxes. One would be entitled, "I can handle this by… " The other would be entitled, "I need help with this." Slips of paper could be written either by the teacher or by the students describing various situations which might arise in the classroom.

The students would then draw a card and place it in the appropriate box. For instance, if the card described a situation of teasing, the student would put the card in the "I can handle this" box and then tell how they might handle the situation without the teacher's intervention. If the student perceives the situation to be dangerous, he/she might place this card in the "I need help with this" box and then explain why the teacher's intervention was necessary.

© 1998, YouthLight, Inc.

If the teacher wanted to make this into a game, the class could be divided into two teams. The teams could draw cards. Each card would have a number of points on it specifically related to the difficulty of the situation. Cards that the teacher would handle would be awarded the least amount of points. A team member would then draw a card and determine whether it was a situation that they thought they could handle or that required adult intervention. If they thought they could handle the situation, the team would be asked to give a means of handling the situation and drop the card in the appropriate box. If the team gives an appropriate response to the situation, they would be awarded the number of points specified on the card. It is important to note that there are no right or wrong answers in this situation. Any attempt towards an appropriate response should be rewarded.

5.   "Match It Up"

The class could be given a matching sheet giving negative situations and appropriate responses to such. The negative situations would be situations which frequently arise in the classroom among students. Responses would be positive to those situations. Such response would be assertive, fair, and independent of adult interference when possible. Some responses may require adult intervention. Examples are as follows:

1. Johnny called Susie "fat."	1. You ask him to stop in a friendly voice. If he refuses, you ask him again in a firmer voice.
2. Mark Keeps tapping his pencil on his desk.	2. She asks him firmly to stop and she moves away from him.
3. Jennifer won't play with Anna at recess.	3. She responds, "I like the way I look."
4. Leon keeps touching Susan's hair.	4. You tell the teacher immediately.
5. Lonnie has a knife in his desk.	5. She asks her to play a game. When she says no, she goes to play with someone else.

All situations usually involve tattling. This matching sheet offers students an opportunity to examine other alternatives for handling problems other than tattling. It also enables students to learn to differentiate those situations which require adult intervention and those which do not.

6.   "Act It Out"

The teacher should give students various situations and ask them to role play these situations. The role play brings an experiential component into learning socials skills, thus increasing the ability to generalize the skill into an actual situation. Some examples of role-play situations are as follows:

1. Johnny says your mother is a "fat slob." What do you do?

© 1998, YouthLight, Inc.

2. Mark stole your pencil. Paula saw him. What do you do?
3. Susan says that you stink. What do you do?
4. Bill hit you in the stomach in the bathroom. What do you do?
5. Lorenzo wants to copy your work. What do you do?
6. Someone touched Suzanne in a way she did not like. What does she do?

Role play encourages students to watch each other handle situations and learn to handle problems on their own. The ultimate goal is to decrease tattling and increase the student's ability to deal with problematic situations.

7. "Friendship Commercials"
Make up a commercial about friends in your group citing many of the positive things about the person. This is especially fun with video cameras or tape recorders. For purposes of this workshop, make up a group commercial to present to the entire group. You may want to focus on your strengths, talents, hobbies, abilities, interests, etc. Presentation should be no more than 45 seconds so that you can tell about your activity. Activity can be processed by discussing how important it is to say positive things about our friends. Building others up instead of putting others down is a skill to learn and develop. You may want to ask how others felt during commercials.

8. "Superhero Capes"
Have children attach a piece of paper, draped like a batman or superman cape to their backs. All children are given markers and asked to silently write positive messages to the children without telling the others what they are writing. At the end of the activity, children can take off their capes and read the comments or ask someone to read the comments for them. For this activity, your group will be using paper plates. Use your imagination and pretend!

9. "Mailbox "
Each child is asked to take one shoe off which will be used for their "mailbox." The "mailboxes" are placed in the center of the circle. Make sure the children have enough small slips of paper so that each child will have enough to write one nice thing about each of the others in the group. After they write the statements, they are asked to put them in the appropriate mailboxes. After everyone is finished, children take turns reading their notes aloud to the group.

10. "Balloon Bop"
Give each child a balloon. Ask them to draw their face on the balloon and write their name on it. Instruct the children to bat the balloons around until you say stop. At this time, children are asked to grab a balloon (preferably not their own). They are then asked to give a compliment to whomever's balloon they are holding. Continue this process several times.

11. "Toilet Paper Pass"
One person is chosen as the leader. Do not read these directions to the group. (You will understand.) Pass around a roll of toilet paper instructing everyone to "take what they need."

© 1998, YouthLight, Inc.

Explain no further and allow people to take off a lot or a little. After this is completed, now explain that for each square of toilet paper, they are to tell one positive thing about themselves. Questions can be varied according to purposes of the group. (See page 126 for a variation of this activity).

12. "Star Finder"

Your group is asked to perform some musical, drama, or other presentation to the large group. You may present your talents, give a skit about things you like to do, sing a rap, recite a poem, etc. If this were in a classroom or small group, each child would be given an opportunity to perform. However, for the sake of time and prevention of embarrassment, you may present as a group. Please try to limit your presentation to about one minute. Thanks. You will be stars and can even make stars if you choose.

13. "Comedy Hour"

This is an activity designed to give kids a chance to share humorous stories or jokes in an appropriate manner. Make a presentation using a few "clean" jokes or humorous stories. Presentation needs to be one minute or less, so that one or two jokes would be fine. Have fun.

© 1998, YouthLight, Inc.

"SHARE"
With Attention-Seeking Students

Remember, children will continue to behave in one particular way until some new behavior is learned. Most students are usually doing the best they can to meet their needs at the time. If "helpers" can provide understanding and support, difficult students can learn new behaviors and how to meet their needs in more effective ways. So, "SHARE" with your students-they can't change alone.

S Show the child how to give and get attention in appropriate ways.

H Humor is something learned. Model and teach appropriate humor.

A Analyze the cause for the behavior. If it is attention, provide the child with appropriate ways to get attention.

R Reinforce appropriate attention-getting behavior. Emphasize the child's strengths and ignore silliness.

E Explore other strategies with the student to meet the goal being achieved through class clowning or teasing. Enlist the group's help through planned ignoring.

© 1998, YouthLight, Inc.

"Refuse the Gossip Game"

PURPOSE:

To teach refusal skills specifically for dealing with gossip.

PROCEDURE:

1. Have students sit in a circle.

2. Teach students the skills of "refusing the gossip."

    A. Use an "I" statement to share your feelings.
        (e.g., "I don't like to say bad things about others.")

    B. Suggest an alternative activity.
        (e.g., "Would you like to go play this game with me?")

3. Have one student be "it" and approach a student in the group and tell some gossip about some-one else in the group that they make up.

4. If the person "refuses" the gossip, that person is applauded by the group.

VARIATION:

The whole group is divided into two teams; each team attempts to accumulate points. Points are earned when team members take turns acting out the gossip and successfully refuse it.

FOLLOW UP:

What different feelings do people have in gossip situations?

What is the peer pressure to participate in gossip?

What are other ways students could help stop gossip?

What are some difficulties students may find when trying to stop gossip?

© 1998, YouthLight, Inc.

"Gossip"

PURPOSE:

To demonstrate how gossip changes and distorts information about people.
To encourage listening skills.

PROCEDURE:

1. Have students sit in a circle.

2. Ask one student to make up a gossip statement about the group or school and whisper it to the person next to him or her. Then, that student whispers the message to the next, and so on.

3. When the last student hears the message, he/she tells the group what it has become (or what it has been changed to).

VARIATION:

Have two students each make up different gossip messages about the group or school. Then, each of these students sits next to each other and passes his or her message on to the next person. As the messages are passed around the circle, they will cross paths and make the activity more interesting. This is what happens when several gossip messages are being passed around at the same time in class.

FOLLOW UP:

What happened to the message as it was passed between several people?

How is this like what happens in "real life"?

How do you explain how "gossip grows"? In other words, when a story is passed around about someone, it seems to get more intense each time it is shared.

© 1998, YouthLight, Inc.

"No Fighting" Game

© 1998, YouthLight, Inc.

PURPOSE:

To teach children appropriate social skills for dealing with problems they are experiencing in the classroom.

TIME:

30 minutes

MATERIALS:

Situation cards, chalkboard

PROCEDURE:

1. Make question cards on small slips of paper reflecting various social situations the students are faced with. These cards become the "problem cards."

2. Assign point values to cards based on the difficulty of the questions. Points could range from "1" to "3." Note: If you are going to have a large game board, use this point system. If you are going to have a small game board, assign all cards a point value of "1."

3. On the blackboard, write the words NO FIGHTING and draw 10 or more blocks under each letter. The boxes would all be numbered down the side. See diagram below.

	N	O	F	I	G	H	T	I	N	G
1										
2										
3										
4										
5										

4. Divide the children up into groups of four. Give each group a name or allow the children to come up with a name.

5. The first group is then allowed to choose up to six cards from the problem card stack. Other groups may choose cards as they have their turns.

6. Each group is given one turn to attempt to solve the problem cards they have just chosen.

7. The cards are handed to the MC (usually the teacher or counselor). If you can find one, use a sand timer or egg timer to give the group a time frame in which to solve the problems on cards.

8. The MC starts the timer and then randomly chooses a card and reads the question. If the team can give an appropriate response to the problem on the card, the team is awarded that number of points. Play continues for that team until time runs out.

9. Numbers of points are then added up and the total is announced for the round. The team is then asked to place their name in a corresponding number of boxes on the game board. For instance, if the teams earned six points, then they are asked to write their team's name in six boxes on the board.

10. Play continues until all groups have played or until the boxes on the board have been filled. It is important to make sure that all teams have a turn.

11. Make sure there are adequate boxes on the board to accommodate the point values on the cards. If you think this might be a problem, you might forego this point system and award one point per each question answered.

12. At the end of the game, the teacher turns his or her back and randomly choose boxes. For instance, H 10, O 9, etc. The teams with their names in these boxes would then be awarded a small prize or be chosen as the winner. The teacher could vary this part of the game. For instance, the first team to be chosen 2 times wins to game.

13. The teacher may also want to throw in questions that purposely require adult intervention to make sure the children can differentiate between situations which do and do not require adult intervention.

VARIATIONS:

Other phrases can be substituted for "no fighting" such as "no tattling," "homework," "on-task," etc. The teacher would write this word on the board and draw blocks underneath the letters as was previously described. Instead of playing a game using questions, the teacher might reward students by asking them to place their initials in blocks for doing or not doing the particular behavior. For example, anyone who brought in homework could put his or her initials in the "Homework" block. Anyone who did not tattle could put their name in the "No tattling" block, etc. At the end of the week or day, prizes could randomly be awarded.

FOLLOW-UP:

The teacher should periodically play the game using different questions dealing with various problems arising in the classroom. Discussion would focus upon the various problems solving strategies and/or solutions students learned while playing the game. The teacher could reinforce these ideas by having a blank game board on the blackboard. Whenever a students used one of these strategies, the student could place their name in one of the blacks, and the teacher could reward the students at the end of the week by random selection.

© 1998, YouthLight, Inc.

"Solving Problems By Myself"

PURPOSE:

To recognize and discuss the consequences of decisions.

TIME:

One session

MATERIALS:

Activity Sheet: *Solving Problems by Myself*
Overhead projector
Transparency of the Activity Sheet

PROCEDURE:

Distribute the Activity Sheet: *Solving Problems by Myself*. Have students choose one of the situations and complete the Activity Sheet individually. Suggest that they think about how other forces around them (other people or circumstances) affect decisions they make.

Wrap-Up

Show a transparency of the Activity Sheet on an overhead. With the whole class, complete the chart for each situation. Encourage students to discuss different decisions they made for the same problem.

© 1998, YouthLight, Inc.

"Solving Problems By Myself"

DIRECTIONS:

Select one situation below and complete the chart about it.

SITUATIONS:

1. My teacher wants me to finish my work and I don't want to.
2. My classmates tease me when I come late to class.
3. I want to check out the same library book as another person.
4. My friend tried to get me to take someone's wallet.
5. Someone pushes me when the teacher leaves the room.
6. Someone accuses me of taking money from a classmate - and I didn't!
7. The record I borrowed from a friend got broken.
8. After lunch, I can't concentrate on my work because I have a headache.
9. I'm trying to work in a noisy classroom.
10. I overhear someone calling my brother a name.

Decision-Making Chart

I choose situation #

When trying to decide what to do...

What are the positive forces?	What are the negative forces?

© 1998, YouthLight, Inc.

"Solving Problems Baseball" Game

PURPOSE:

To teach problem solving skills in dealing with social situations.

To demonstrate that there are always several ways of dealing with problems.

To give a visual demonstration that focusing on solutions actually moves one closer to solving the problem.

PROCEDURE:

1. Divide the children into two teams.

2. Make bases and place them in appropriate order to represent home, 1st, 2nd, and 3rd base. Place three boxes in the outfield.

3. Make problem cards depicting various social situations children are faced with. Place 1/3 of all problem cards into each of the three boxes in the outfield.

4. The first child to "bat comes up to home base. This child has tree chance to throw the ball into one of the boxes in outfield. If the child throws the ball into one of the boxes, the child is allowed to choose one of the questions from one of the boxes. If the child is unable to get the ball into one of the outfield boxes, the team loses their turn. The throws are considered "strikes".

5. The MC or teacher reads the question and checks to see if the student and team understand the question.

6. A sand time is used to keep time and is turned over when the team indicates that they are ready to begin.

7. The team's job is to think of four alternative responses to this particular problem that might be appropriate. As the teams think of one appropriate response, the batter is moved to first base. As the teams think of a second appropriate response, the team moves to second. A third response moves the team to third and the final response moves the team to home. If the team is able to think of four responses before the timer runs out, the team is awarded a run. Play then goes to the other team.

8. To provide order for this process, the moving player is asked to call on team mates for answers rather than randomly asking for answers. The MC must be able to hear the response for the response to be acceptable.

© 1998, YouthLight, Inc.

9. At the end of the inning or run, the moving player is then asked which response or she might choose as a response to the problem.

10. Play continues as time allows.

11. The teacher or counselor may want to process the information by suggesting that for every problem, there are always many things you can do. The challenge is merely to brainstorm various solutions to get you "unstuck".

© 1998, YouthLight, Inc.

"Line It Up"

PURPOSE:

To teach children acceptable ways of dealing with social situations.

PROCEDURE:

1. Three rows of three chairs are set up in a central location in the classroom.

2. The teacher makes 5 cards with an X on them and 5 with an O on them.

3. The teacher makes problem cards with questions describing various social situations that the children might find themselves in.

4. Children are divided into two teams. Teams choose either the X's or the O's and are given those cards.

5. One child is chosen to start. This child chooses a question and the MC (teacher) asks the question. If the child gets the question right, the child is asked to choose a chair and sit in it with either their X or O.

6. Play continues until one team has tic tac toe.

FOLLOW-UP:

Discussion focuses on what was learned from answering the questions, and how these situations can be integrated into the classroom. The teacher could encourage students to work on implementing the strategies and give verbal reinforcement when a student does implement a particular strategy.

VARIATIONS:

Questions can be changed according to problems arising in the classroom. Questions may also be directed towards the curriculum -- in particular, areas which involve interpersonal conflict. Using the curriculum, students can not only cover subject matter, but also give the opportunity to brainstorm solutions to interpersonal problems.

© 1998, YouthLight, Inc.

"Go Fishing"

PURPOSE:

To teach children appropriate means of dealing with social situations.

PROCEDURE:

Game One:

1. The teacher makes a "pond" to be placed on the floor.

2. The teacher makes little fish cards which are laid face down in the pond. Some fish have numbers on them. Some fish have a star on them signifying that the student who chooses that particular fish gets a prize. One or two fish might say everyone gets a prize. All fish have magnets on them.

3. The teacher makes a fishing pole with a magnet attached to a string on the end of the pole.

4. The teacher makes a social skills questions list, numbered one to thirty (or however many fish there will be in the pond.)

5. Children take turns going fishing. Each child goes fishing by throwing the fishing pole in the water and catching a fish. If the child catches a fish with a number on the card, they are asked to answer the question which corresponds with the number.

6. For a variation, the class can be divided into teams and point values placed on the fish. Not only can the children answer the questions, but they can see which teams accumulate the most points. To get the points, the question must be answered appropriately.

7. Play continues until time runs out or until each child has had a turn.

Game Two:

1. There are two fishing ponds. One with problem "fish" and one with "answer" fish. This becomes a matching and concentration game. Again the problems would reflect social skills questions.

2. Divide the class into two teams.

© 1998, YouthLight, Inc.

3. One person is chosen to begin and goes fishing for a problem fish. The team then gets three chances to go fishing in the "answers" pond to come up with an appropriate solution to the "problem." If the team can appropriately justify a particular response, it is counted as a match. A match is awarded 10 points for the team.

4. Should a team not get an appropriate response in their three chances, they can hold the card until next time. Hopefully, by paying attention, they may see the other team overturn an appropriate answer.

5. Play continues until one team gets 100, until both teams get 50, or until the teacher says stop.

FOLLOW-UP:

Discussion focuses on various situations found on the "fish" cards and how students might implement one strategy during the next week. In addition, the teacher could follow up by making a bulletin board with fish on the board. Whenever students implemented a strategy, their name and successful behavior could be written on the board. This would reinforce positive behaviors noted during the week.

© 1998, YouthLight, Inc.

"Crater Cross"

PURPOSE:

To help children to affirm each other.

To help children learn to think positively about their own strengths and abilities.

PROCEDURE:

1. Divide children into two teams. Place 8 or 9 craters in the middle of the two teams. Craters can be pieces of paper or old crates.

2. One child is chosen to cross the craters. The child has to step on each of the crater as he/she crosses the river.

3. Position the child on the first crater and turn the sand timer over. During this time period, the child who is moving must choose a team member to say something positive or affirming to him or her before he/she can move to the next crater.

4. The child wins if he/she can cross the craters before the time runs out. The team is awarded 25 points for each child who crosses the crater.

5. To make it more challenging, a ball can be added. The "moving" child throws the ball to a team member from the crater. The team member who catches the ball is then asked to compliment the moving player. If either of the players drop the ball, the player must start all over again. This aspect encourages team cooperation and seems to make everyone pay better attention to the game.

FOLLOW-UP:

The students can be asked to tell how they felt to affirm others and think positively about themselves during the activity. Students might also be asked to commit to saying a certain number of statements about themselves or others during the next few days. To reinforce this further, the teacher could do other activities which might include writing in journals, playing the balloon bop, doing the mailbox activity and/or others found in this book.

© 1998, YouthLight, Inc.

"Talking Behind Your Back"

PURPOSE:

To show that children can write affirming comments literally "behind someone's back."

PROCEDURE:

1. Tape a piece of construction paper to each student's back.

2. Talk to the students about ground rules. These rules should include no put downs or inappropriate comments. Should a student choose to break any of these rules, they would automatically be suspended from the game.

3. Write several appropriate comments or phrases on the board to help with spelling and to help the students begin to think of comments they could write.

4. Ask the students to mingle around the room writing positive comments on each other's backs.

5. Ask the students to stop once the game has gone on for a few minutes or the students have had time to obtain several comments on the pieces of paper on their backs. Ask the students to sit in a circle.

6. Once the students are in a circle, the instructor should randomly ask a student for a number between 1 and 10.

7. A student is chosen to begin. Depending on the number chosen, the student would then count this many children and read the paper on that child's back. For example, if 6 were chosen, the person would read the 6th person's paper. The "walking" student would then take the "sitting" person's place and the "sitting" person would become the "walking" person.

FOLLOW-UP:

This game is directed in a positive manner and students could be asked to discuss how they felt while playing. Students will usually answer positively and thus they can be challenged to utilize this concept in the classroom. The teacher might even challenge the class to tell him or her in a class meeting that someone affirmed them in some way during the week. Students could be urged to talk positively about their friends.

© 1998, YouthLight, Inc.

"Duck, Duck Friend"

PURPOSE:

To teach children how to affirm each other.

PROCEDURE:

1. Students are asked to sit in a circle. One child is chosen as "it."

2. "It" walks around the circle tapping each student on the head. As this student touches another student on the head, they say a compliment to the child whose head is being touched.

3. Whenever the student is ready to have someone chase him or her, he/she merely taps someone on the head and says "friend."

4. The child chosen as "friend" then gets up and chases the student around the circle. If the student makes it around the circle without getting caught, the other student becomes "it." If the running student is caught, he/she must sit in the mushpot. If a student goes in the mushpot, the class can sing them a little I love you song to get them out.

FOLLOW-UP:

Discussion focuses on the importance of affirmation in dealing with friends. Students could be challenged to begin saying these statements during classroom time and verbally reinforced whenever they were heard saying positive statements.

© 1998, YouthLight, Inc.

"What I Can Do" Book

PURPOSE:

To encourage children to draw or write things they are able to do or are successful with.

PROCEDURE:

1. This project can be done either individually or as a group. Children are asked to draw pictures of things they can do.

2. Once pictures are drawn, the instructor can help the child put these into book form.

3. Books can be placed at reading centers for all to read.

VARIATIONS:

Students can make books of subjects they are good in, talents they have, what they would like to be when they grow up, etc. Each student could be responsible for one page and each page might become part of a book. This would serve to help students feel good about themselves, learn about their friends, and become connected with the group.

FOLLOW-UP:

Discussion could focus on appreciating others' talents, taking time to understand people and appreciating others. The teacher could play guessing games with the information in the book thus helping students feel important and valued in the classroom.

© 1998, YouthLight, Inc.

"Musical Dress Up"

PURPOSE:

Children learn to say positive things about themselves.

PROCEDURE:

1. Fill a large trash bag with various "silly" dress up items. These might include hats, scarves, gloves, necklaces, glasses, long skirts, wigs, mouse ears, etc.

2. Children are asked to sit in a circle. As the music starts, the bag is passed around the circle. When the music stops, the student has 5 seconds to say something positive about themselves. If they are unable to do it, they have to reach into the bag and put on whatever they pull out.

3. Students are declared winners at the end of the game if they have not had to "dress up."

FOLLOW-UP:

Students are asked how they can "think fast" throughout the day to prevent them from looking "silly" in front of their friends. Discussion may focus on study habits, homework, peer pressure, or behavior. Students need to realize they are often called upon to make "split second" decisions in each of these areas. The wrong decision may cause them to face an unpleasant consequence in front of peers, family, or teachers.

© 1998, YouthLight, Inc.

"Musical Moves"

PURPOSE:

To teach children to give affirming statements to each other.

PROCEDURE:

1. Children are asked to sit in a circle.

2. The music is started and children begin to throw or roll the ball to each other.

3. Whenever the music stops, the child who is holding the ball has 10 seconds to call on three people to give them compliments. If a called on person is unable to give the compliment in time, they are out of the game. (Note: usually children are able to do this in plenty of time. However, if there seems to be a problem, extend the time a bit. The goal is for the children to be successful.)

4. Play continues as long as the leader desires.

FOLLOW-UP:

Students would be encouraged to think of responses quickly which would be affirming in nature. The teacher might ask the students to describe how they felt both giving compliments responding to friends accomplishments as well. Free activity is designed to help the student learn to "think" fast in a positive manner about his or her friends.

© 1998, YouthLight, Inc.

Class Clowns

Class Clowns are students attempting to meet their need for attention by acting silly or foolish. Children may meet their needs for love and belonging, fun, and power by using this behavior. Remember, what did Charlie Chaplin, W.C. Fields, Cid Ceaser, Ernie Covacs, Freddi Prince, Jacki Gleason, and John Belushi have in common? These famous comedians and many more used their comedy, in part, to help them cope with deep troubles in their lives.

Characteristics:

1. They attempt to use humor to distract others in the classroom.

2. They may play "practical" jokes on others.

3. They may make distorted faces or make frequent unexpected comments.

4. They may display attention-seeking gestures or sounds such as giggling or simulating body sounds.

Underlying Causes:

1. They may believe they have no better way to solicit attention.

2. They may have feelings of low self-worth or confidence and may be seeking recognition.

3. They may have never learned appropriate humor.

4. They may be attempting to divert attention away from family problems such as alcohol abuse or family violence.

5. They may be attempting to cope with a class that is frustrating or boring to them.

Strategies:

1. Teach children appropriate humor by pointing out how things are funny to you.

2. Let the class clown know that you appreciate his or her humor, but make sure the child knows his or her "serious" side is also appreciated and important.

3. Give the student a chance to "shine" as a comic at a specified time.

4. Use "Attention Redirection." For example, develop a plan with the student that will help the child meet his or her comic needs, yet control them.

5. Help the child understand his or her need for attention and help find other ways, in addition to humor, to receive this attention.

© 1998, YouthLight, Inc.

6. Provide the child tasks that require intensive concentration.

7. Redirect the child's creative talents through activities like dramatics, games, and puppets.

8. Even if all the other students continue to laugh at the "class clown", don't overly react yourself.

9. Place the child in situations in which he/she can gain appropriate attention from peers.

10. Allow children to be in leadership positions.

11. Use seldom-tapped resources such as peer helpers and/or mentors to help the class clown to receive attention in the form of personal listening, affirming, and/or participative learning activities.

Helpful hints for Dealing with "Class Clowns"

1. Build into your schedule release times when it is OK to be the class clown without censure.

2. Give the clown responsibility that demands concentration. Find an isolated place for him to work. The task should make him feel important as well as convince him that you take him seriously.

3. Interpret the clown's goals for him. ("You crave attention and you feel clowning is the best way to get it.")

4. Praise the student about something that carries the inference that he's sensitive, not just a clown.

5. Preempt and redirect the student's disposition to clown.

© 1998, YouthLight, Inc.

"The Clown Game"

PURPOSE:

The purpose of the "Clown Game" is to teach children appropriate and inappropriate means of getting attention. Children will be encouraged in a fun way to learn to discriminate ways to get attention. This can be transformed into a classroom game in which the teacher could have a bulletin board with a clown and a lot of juggling balls.

As the children exhibit appropriate means of getting attention, the teacher can write the behavior and the child's name on the board. When the board is filled up, perhaps the class could earn an afternoon of playing ball or a party with a clown (perhaps a parent could dress up).

PROCEDURE:

1. Draw a big picture of a clown which could be colored by participants.

2. Draw balls on another page which children could cut out. Cut out the circles and attach a piece of Velcro to each.

3. Write examples of appropriate and inappropriate ways of getting attention on the circles. Examples are:

4. Say, "Clowns get a lot of attention by doing silly things in the circus and are paid to do this. We need to get attention too. Place the circles with appropriate means of getting attention beside the clown."

- Hitting Someone
- Asking your friend to share your snack
- Putting food all over your mouth
- Pinching your neighbor
- Punching your friend
- Interrupting the teacher

- Asking someone to play with you
- Telling a joke at recess
- Playing chase with your friend recess
- Laughing out loud while the teacher is teaching
- Getting your name on the board
- Talking to your neighbor while the teacher is teaching

FOLLOW UP:

Have students pair up and brainstorm lists of appropriate and inappropriate ways to get attention while:
- Doing chores at home.
- Reading silently in class.
- Taking a bath.
- Waiting for your food in a restaurant.
- Standing in a crowd of people you don't know.

Discuss why it is important for us to get attention from others.

© 1998, YouthLight, Inc.

"Attention Circles"

PURPOSE:

To help children distinguish between appropriate and inappropriate ways of getting attention.

PROCEDURE:

1. Draw about a 12-inch diameter circle on a sheet of tagboard or poster board.

2. Cut the circle out and punch about 12 pencil-sized holes around the circle, each about 1-inch from the outer rim of the circle.

3. Randomly print an appropriate or inappropriate way to seek attention next to each hole.

4. For each appropriate answer, turn the circle over and draw a star around the hole.

5. Have one student hold the circle so another can read the items.

6. Then, have him or her stick a pencil through each hole, one at a time, that shows an appropriate way to seek attention. The student holding the circle should watch the back side of the card and can easily tell if the answer is correct or not. A correct answer is when the pencil pokes through a star.

FOLLOW UP:

Allow students to create other shapes.

Ask students to brainstorm other ideas for appropriate ways to get attention.

© 1998, YouthLight, Inc.

Source Unknown

Manipulators
"Truth Benders" & "Game Players"

Manipulators deliberately misgive information or misguide someone to achieve some predictable payoff. Players become increasingly adept with practice and confident with success.

Manipulators often need power and want control. They have a goal in mind of how they want other people to behave or believe. Skilled players develop back-up plans.

© 1998, YouthLight, Inc.

Truth Benders

Characteristics:

1. They may make untrue statements which are either:
    • a simple reversal of the truth.
    • an exaggeration (magnification of the truth).
    • a fabrication (creation of an untrue story).
    • a confabulation (development of a story that is partly true and partly false).
    • a wrong accusation (blaming on someone else).

2. They have an intent to deceive to gain personal advantage or to avoid unpleasantness.

3. All children make untrue statements on occasion. According to Piaget, children have three stages of lying.
    <u>Stage 1</u>:   The child believes the lie is wrong because it is punished.
    <u>Stage 2</u>:   The lie becomes "wrong" even without the punishment.
    <u>Stage 3</u>:   The lie is wrong because it is in conflict with mutual respect and affection.

Underlying Causes:

1. Lying is an index to a child's feelings of being unloved or from feelings of inadequacy and pressure.

2. They may attempt to enhance themselves in front of others by claiming to do things which actually may not have occurred.

3. They may hope to gain the attention and approval of others.

4. They may strive to maintain friendships with other children.

5. They may be trying to get revenge on other children.

6. They may be attempting to fulfill expectations of significant adults who have labeled them as a "liar."

7. They may be striving to imitate the examples of other significant adults who may lie to avoid confrontations with others or to gain some positions as a result of such.

© 1998, YouthLight, Inc.

8. They may be attempting to escape dealing with painful memories or occurrences from the past.

9. They may be following modeled family values.

Strategies:

1. Confront the behavior based on the evidence at hand, making a statement to the child about the behavior. Do not demand that children testify against themselves by insisting on a confession. When questioned too harshly, children may feel that it is necessary to keep lying to avoid punishment.

2. Role model honestly by admitting openly to the children when you make mistakes. Be sure children trust in your honesty with them.

3. Teach honesty as an important virtue or value of daily living. Provide stories, dramatics, or puppets that illustrate the power of truthfulness.

4. Resist the temptation to moralize or preach because the child will "tune you out."

5. Convey the idea that you are more willing to remember the times a child told the truth than the times he/she lied.

6. Maintain a safe and encouraging classroom climate in which children are allowed to express ideas and make mistakes without fear.

7. Apply consequences cautiously for lying. It may be appropriate to include two consequences, one for the misdeed, and one for the lie, but be careful not to be too intense.

8. In the case of extreme exaggerations, do not react too much, but remember what was said. Listen especially to the feelings behind the exaggeration. These stories are the child's attempts to communicate some underlying needs to you.

9. Provide positive reinforcement for truthful acts.

10. Help children who bend the truth by using problem-solving techniques. If a child desires attention, brainstorm appropriate ways to gain attention. If a child desires to protect his or her friends, don't ask that child to be the sole discloser of facts. If a child fears failure, give the child adequate room to succeed.

© 1998, YouthLight, Inc.

Helpful Hints for Dealing with "Truth Benders"

1. Assure the child that he can depend upon you to tell him the truth.

2. Convey the idea that you are more willing to remember the times he told the truth than the times he lied. ("Phil, I'm sure it was difficult for you to admit you forgot to tell your dad to call me last night, but I'm so proud of you for admitting it." The assumption here is that the teacher and the student recognize the problem and are both working on it.)

3. Deal directly with the habitual liar instead of trying to trap him. ("Jim, you have Carrie's purse. Please return it to her.")

4. Evaluate your expectations of the student and try to discern the areas in which he feels compelled to lie. Does he, for example, lie about schoolwork? His dad's job? His mother's job? His wardrobe? His physical prowess?

5. Ignore those fantasy-oriented tales that probably have no serious consequences. ("My grandpa gives me $5.00 every time I go to see him." Even though you know his grandpa is on welfare, pass this up. Ignore it, but remember it for what it is.)

6. Read or tell stories that illustrate the power of truthfulness over falsehoods. Resist the temptation to moralize, because as soon as you do, you'll be tuned out.

7. Use normal consequences to help the student learn the benefits of telling the truth. ("You said you had finished and it's clear you didn't tell the truth; so you will have to forego the pleasure of _____.")

© 1998, YouthLight, Inc.

"Lies"

PURPOSE:

To discuss "lies" that we see in the media and how they influence our lives.

To begin looking carefully at the messages sent to us from the media and the values they portray.

PROCEDURE:

1. Cut out pictures of advertisements and write on tagboard.
   Laminate.   Examples:
   - A. People drinking in a van with a lot of friends, having a lot of fun.
   - B. Your brain is like an egg. This is what happens when you're on drugs - the egg fries.
   - C. The tidy bowl man.
   - D. The Nestea plunge
   - E. Starburst
   - F. Nike Air commercial.

2. After each picture, the student is asked what the commercial implies. e.g., "If you drink beer, you'll have lots of friends and have lots of fun."

3. Is that the truth or an illusion? If it is an illusion as is the example above, what is the real underlying truth? (e.g., "If you drink too much, alcohol will damage your body, impair your ability to drive, impair your judgment, etc.)

FOLLOW UP:

Talk about what kind of lies most people try to believe.

1. I must wear Calvin Klein jeans.
2. I must have Nike Air.
3. I need Bugle Boys.
4. I must drink to have friends and to have fun.

What would happen if each of us told 10 lies each day?

Are all lies wrong or bad? Give an example to defend your point of view.

© 1998, YouthLight, Inc.

"What If?"

PURPOSE:

To motivate students to think proactively.
To think ahead about possible consequences for their actions.

PROCEDURE:

1. Make ten to fifteen cards with different numbers of points written on them. For example, some cards could have 25, 50, and 100 points, and perhaps one with 200 points.

2. Divide the class into two teams and give each team one bean bag.

3. Place the cards, with numbers showing, randomly in the middle of the floor.

4. One child throws his or her team's bag so that it lands on or near one point card.

5. Then, this child draws one question card from a pile of "What If . . ." questions such as:

   • What if you accidentally broke a neighbor's window while playing ball? What would you do?

   • What if you returned home and found you had accidentally kept your friend's five dollar bill that you found. What would you do?

   • What if you heard that someone was telling lies about you in the classroom. What would you do?

   • What if you found out that you won a new sports car in a contest, but had to be 21 years old to get it. What would you do?

   • What if someone said he/she was going to beat you up after school and wanted to know which way you were going home. What would you do?

6. The game continues as time allows. When finished, emphasize that no team really lost.

FOLLOW UP:

• Discuss the importance of honesty.
• Discuss whether or not you should <u>always</u> be honest in every situation, no matter what.
• Explore what happens if you are caught in a lot of lies by someone.

© 1998, YouthLight, Inc.

"Yes" or "No" Game

PURPOSE:

To identify behaviors in children that indicate good social skills.

PROCEDURE:

1. Make a large game board with 6 boxes across and 6 boxes down.

2. Make a pocket over each box that is big enough to hold one question.

3. Make 36 yes or no questions and put them in the pockets.

4. The object of the game will be to get 6 yes answers or no answers in a row either vertically, horizontally, or diagonally. Therefore, questions will need to be strategically placed. Place at least 3 rows of yes or no answers. The game is won when all three rows are found.

5. Make 2 different colors of cards to place in the pockets. One will signify yes answers and the other no answers. One card will be placed in each pocket after the question has been answered.

6. Ask a child to come up and choose a card and answer the card. They are asked to place the corresponding card in the pocket to indicate the correct answer to the question.

7. Children are asked to look for patterns.

8. Play continues until game is won by finding all 3 rows.

FOLLOW-UP:

Discussion focuses on helping students learn positive behaviors that help them grow socially, emotionally, and academically. Continually pointing out the pluses may help bring these positive behaviors into a student's quality world. Such behavior can enable students to feel more success both personally and academically. Any means of reinforcement of positive work habits is certainly a plus.

© 1998, YouthLight, Inc.

"Shoot the Hoop"

PURPOSE:

To help children brainstorm character building traits.

PROCEDURE:

1.   Divide the children into small groups.

2.   Ask them to brainstorm positive character building traits and jot these down. Examples might include being honest, studying hard, being respectful, etc.

3.   For each positive character trait the group comes up with, the group gets one shot with a nerf® basketball.

4.   Each completed shot is worth 1 or 2 points (leader's choice). The group who wins is the group that gets the most points for their shots.

FOLLOW-UP:

Discussion would be centered around the benefits of utilizing the character building traits. Students might be asked to consider "what's in it for them" if they act in this manner. The teacher might ask the students to jot down one character building trait they would like to work on and a plan for developing it.

© 1998, YouthLight, Inc.

"Stick Together"

PURPOSE:

To help children identify positive characteristics that help them "stick" together with friends.

PROCEDURE:

1. Make a list of characteristics that either enhance or break down friendships. For example, sharing might enhance a friendship whereas hitting may break down a friendship. Put these characteristics on cards and place them in a basket.

2. Ask one student at a time to choose a card out of a basket with all cards inside.

3. The student is asked to identify whether the trait is a "sticking together" trait or a pulling apart trait. If the trait is a stick together trait, the student is asked to stand up and place his or her arms in the air. The teacher or counselor then wraps masking tape around the child's waist.

4. Other children are called to choose a card. Each time a positive trait is drawn, the children are asked to stand beside the "taped" student as you tape this student to the previous student. This usually works better if the students face in opposite directions.

5. Play continues until 7 or 8 students are taped together. The students are then asked to walk together to a destination that you have previously designated. They are told that they must walk without breaking the tape. If they are able to work together to accomplish this goal, they are declared winners.

FOLLOW-UP:

The teacher or counselor might then take the opportunity to suggest that as long as the group is doing appropriate things, then it is O.K. to stick with this group. However, once someone determines to steal, seriously hurt someone, or cheat on tests, then one might want to break away or pull apart from the group. The teacher or counselor might want to discuss the difficulty of pulling away from friends due to tremendous peer pressure.

One other thing that might happen is the tape may break at some point. The kids may look at you for what to do. This might be a good opportunity to discuss mending friendships, the importance of apologies, and accepting responsibility when things go wrong. Tape can be pieced back together; friendships are often more difficult. Therefore, children need to learn the importance of being careful with friends.

© 1998, YouthLight, Inc.

Game Players

Game Players are children who are attempting to meet their need for power and perhaps even love, belonging, and fun. They are adept at finding ways to control people and at learning which buttons to push to get what they want.

Characteristics:

These are children who:
- seek to dominate others.
- seek to play games by manipulating others.
- blame others for their problems.
- feel frustrated, angry and unloved when others will not behave as they want them to.
- complain and whine to get what they want. (very dependent children)

Underlying Causes:

They may play games to:
- protect themselves.
- get what they want.
- get out of doing things.
- cover up a perceived weakness.
- avoid being responsible.
- keep from looking bad or foolish.
- get other people to solve their problems.
- avoid an unpleasant situation.
- look good in front of others.
- get attention.
- avoid being asked.
- place blame on others so it won't be placed on you.
- be "better" than others.
- be pitied and "victims."
- prove how tough and/or wonderful they are.
- look important.
- get their way.
- get help.
- have others worry about them.
- get sympathy.

Strategies:

1. Present the concept of "con games" to children and differentiate these games from those that are more positive, like sports and board games. For example, "con-games" are plans that we might make to "trick" people into doing or not doing something. They are not honest.

2. Define and give examples of games.
   - acting tired to get out of doing the dishes.
   - acting busy so as not to have to talk to someone.
   - acting afraid to keep from trying something new.
   - acting like a bully to prevent others from knowing how afraid we really are.

74

© 1998, YouthLight, Inc.

3. Become "game-wise" and help students "restructure" their games.

4. Allow students to share games they have played with others.

5. Help students to learn to recognize their own games.

6. Help students to realize how they use games in various situations in front of various people.

7. Help students to realize how games help them get what they want or need from other situations. For example, games may help them manipulate others so that they can receive more love or attention or receive power and/or revenge.

8. Confront the student's game, state the behavior, and ask students if they would be willing to do the activity without the specific game.

9. Determine which games might be appropriate and which games might not.

10. Ask students to think of what things they want, for example, attention from teachers and having friends. Ask them to cut out of a magazine what they can do to get what they want. Students could also draw what they will have to do to get what they want in appropriate ways.

11. Ask students to create their own collages of what they want and/or need. Discuss with students needs such as for love, acceptance, safety, and fun. Ask them to make a list of their needs, and then to choose three. Then ask them to draw and/or write lists of ways in which they can meet their needs.

12. Video tape or audio tape several games and let the students tell you what they're about.

13. Make puppets or masks to demonstrate games to others.

14. Watch a TV clip and point out "games."

© 1998, YouthLight, Inc.

"Becoming Game-Wise"

If the Game is:	The Underlying Need May Be:	A Suggested Intervention
Temper Tantrums	Power over adults; getting what the student wants.	Ignoring the behavior; time-out; not rewarding the behavior.
"Cool"	Power, attention, looking good in front of others.	Acknowledge the student for appropriate actions.
Helpless	To avoid being asked to do things; dependency probably inadvertently reinforced by adults in the student's life.	Encourage the student to complete the task. Do not buy into the "helpless" act. Reward the student for completing tasks. (May use a behavior contract.)
Bullying	To look important; To look "better" than others. The need for power. The need to mask insecurity. Anger about some issues. Poor social skills learned from a violent home.	Conflict resolution. Examine underlying causes (determine if a family intervention is necessary.) Teach social skills; reward peaceful resolutions to problems. (May want to use a behavior contract.)
"Don't Care"	Insecurity - fear of failure. To achieve recognition of self-worth.	Set up success identity - utilize motivational strategies. Re-ward any successful behaviors. Allow the student to be a helper to teach peers. Also, encourage positive self-evaluation.
Clowning	Attention from others, love and belonging, need for fun, masking a family problem like alcoholism.	Allow the student to gain attention in appropriate ways. Have a star search, comedy hour, etc. in the classroom. Reward appropriate behavior.
Stubborn	Power, freedom, testing the adult's ability for giving consequences.	Give student choices; do not allow the student to maintain control over the adult. Provide a choice with one being a natural consequence for continued behavior.

© 1998, YouthLight, Inc.

If the Game is:	The Underlying Need May Be:	A Suggested Intervention
I Can't	Avoidance of responsibility, dependency, fear of failure (probably reinforced by adults).	Do not allow the student to get by without doing the task. Do not buy into the attitude. Do not help the student every step of the way. Reward the student for trying. May want to use an "I Can."
Fearful	May indicate some traumatic situations. May use at home to control others. May use to avoid an unpleasant situation. May use to cover up weakness.	Acknowledge feeling; explore family situation if you are suspicious. Use rehearsal techniques and allow student to practice handling the fearful situation in a safe environment. Relaxation techniques.
Whining	Attention, power, feeling bad (needs not met).	Ignore, time-out, make sure needs are met.
Name-Calling	Need to elevate self; power over others; lack of appropriate social skills; attention.	Notice positive behavior; time-out; encourage empathy, teach social skills.
Cutesy	Attention from adults and/or other students.	Give student attention for appropriate behavior; Allow student to help others.
Blamer	Fearful of consequences; avoidance of responsibility; power.	Reward responsible behaviors; do not buy into the blame; allow the student to accept responsibility for providing a consequence for his or her behavior.

© 1998, YouthLight, Inc.

Restructuring Student "Games"

S State the current behavior or what the child is actually doing.

T Talk to the child about the preferred or desired behavior.

O Offer the child choices.

P Provide a consequence for continued misbehavior.

This model is a way of dealing with manipulative behavior. For example, if a child is whining, you might say the following:

1. State the behavior:	"Johnny, it sounds like you are whining."
2. Talk to the child about the preferred behavior:	"I would like for you to speak to me in your regular voice and tell me what you want."
3. Offer choices:	"If you would like to talk to me in your normal voice, we can talk and you can stay in the classroom. If you continue to whine, you can choose time-out for 10 minutes (varies depending on age of child) Which would you like?"
4. Provide a consequence:	If Johnny chooses to continue whining, the latter consequence would immediately be provided.

Note that if "STOP" doesn't change the unwanted behavior in the other student, then there needs to be a back up plan, such as just walking away, or telling a teacher.

© 1998, YouthLight, Inc.

"Match It Up"

> ## PURPOSE:
>
> To help students begin to identify games and begin having insight
> into their own behaviors.

PROCEDURE:

1. Make a game board out of tagboard. Use the categories of game players we have provided below, or make up your own.

2. If time, have students draw, or cut out a picture from a magazine for each category. Paste these on the board in random order and label each.
   - bully
   - clown
   - name caller
   - fearful
   - cool
   - stubborn
   - truth bender
   - blamer
   - too tired
   - too busy
   - I can't

3. On another sheet, print and cut out phrases which are representative of the different kinds of game players.
   For example,
   - "I'll beat your head into the ground!"
   - "Do you want to hear something funny?"
   - "You are so dumb!"
   - "I can't do this math, its too hard for me."
   - "I'm the baddest kid in this school!"
   - "You can't make me!"

4. Students are asked to match the statements with the pictures. They may place the statements on top of the board if used with a small group or use Velcro if playing with a large group.

FOLLOW UP:

Discuss the following topics:
- A time they experienced someone playing that game.

- Which games have they played? What happened?

- The fact that we all play games sometimes.

- Sometimes games may be okay, sometimes they may not.

- We don't have to play games. It is okay to say what we want and to be who we are.

© 1998, YouthLight, Inc.

"Stop the Behavior" Game

PURPOSE:

To teach children a method to help them learn to confront other children when they are playing games.

PROCEDURE:

1. Ask children to sit in a circle.

2. Depending on the age of the children, discuss several kinds of con-games that children play with each other.

3. Explain the **STOP** method (See previous page).

4. Make a card for each game type listing the game, and perhaps including a drawing or symbol in a basket.

5. Children may take turns picking one of the game cards from the basket.

6. When it is a child's turn, he/she chooses another student and acts out the game with him or her.

7. The student who is receiving the game is asked to use the "STOP" method. For example, Jane chose the "bully" card and acted it out on Susie. Susie then:
   - State the behavior: "Jane, you're pushing me around and acting like a bully."
   - Talk about the desired behavior: "I would like it if you would play catch with me."
   - Offer a choice: "If you would like to play catch, I will play with you. If not, I will go play with someone else."
   - Provide the follow through with the consequence. In this case, Jane continued pushing her, so Susie just walked away.

VARIATION:

You may use a red stop sign to help reinforce the idea.

FOLLOW UP:

After each role play, you might encourage a discussion about other options.

© 1998, YouthLight, Inc.

Hostile Students
"Sherman Tanks," "Snipers," & "Exploders"

Hostile students are those attempting to meet their need for power. Most hostile or aggressive acts are attempts to communicate feelings of hurt and inner pain. Some may express revenge or be a part of the grief and loss process. They are powerful because their behavior arouses confusion, mental or physical flight, and a sense of helpless frustration and leads to tears or rage. These acts rob the victim of the ability to deal with the situation calmly and competently.

Hostile students may take various forms. Aggression may be provoked or unprovoked or may take the form of a tantrum. Aggression may be physical or psychological or both.

© 1998, YouthLight, Inc.

Nine Tips on Being Angry and Fighting Fair

When you feel angry you can:

1. Imagine a sign in front of our eyes. Put a stop to your growing anger. This may mean taking a deep breath, or walking away for a few minutes.

2. Identify your feelings to yourself. Ask yourself some important questions: What am I really angry about? Do I have a good reason to be angry with the other person, or have I been looking for an excuse to hurt him or her? Am I picking a fight because I'm in a bad mood? Or am I really mad at someone else but afraid to let that person know?

3. If you feel that you have to argue, make sure you choose your time and place carefully. Don't try to resolve arguments when you've got to go to class or you're about to eat lunch. If the other person persists, you might answer, "Look   (person's name), this is too important for both of us to spend only a few minutes on. I think we both need time to talk and listen. And even if you don't feel you need the time, I do. Let's meet after school when we have more time to talk."

4. When you do begin to talk with the other person with whom you have a problem, express your feelings without losing control of them. Use words like "I feel . . ." Do not raise your voice or move toward them in a threatening way. Stay calm.

5. Once you're talking, stick to one issue at a time. Don't tell them about their "momma . . ." It really does not help to use phrases like: "Yo mamma wears combat boots, Yo big head, You weak, scoop-up head, or "peasey head." When you really want to straighten out the argument, **stick to the issue**. Don't blame or accuse the other person.

6. Express your point of view. Use the word "I." For example, instead of saying "YOU never listen to me," you might say, "I feel I'm not being listened to when I talk."

7. The secret of fair fighting is arguing not to win, but to seek resolution that works for both of you. You don't have to win - and see the other person lose - to get results. Both parties win of you can keep your self-esteem in a fight and learn something from it. For example, you don't have to call your friend names to let him know that it hurts to be stood up. Letting your friend know how you feel can help him change.

8. **Listen carefully to everything the other person has to say!** If your friend tells you she is late because she always comes by your house to get you, it may be time to meet halfway between her house and yours.

9. **Forgive . . .** once the argument is over. Forgiving is letting go of the anger that sparked the fight. Then a handshake, or hug, is a good way to end an argument. **Get on with your life.**

© 1998, YouthLight, Inc.

How to Handle
Conflicts Constructively

There are three ways to deal with anger:

1. You can "stuff it." But if you stuff or hide anger, you may become withdrawn or depressed. And one day you might explode.

2. You can "escalate it." But if you blow up, blame others, and call them names, your anger has a good chance of working up into violence. That's the worst way to handle your feelings.

3. You can "direct it." When you say to someone, for example, "I feel angry when you're late," you're directing your anger squarely and taking responsibility not only for resolving the conflict, but for making yourself feel better.

**Even if you have problems with your anger, . . .
You can still learn to fight fair and get results**

Group assignment: Each member of the class writes one sentence describing one thing that happened recently which made the class member angry:

Sentence: _____

_____

Volunteers read their sentence aloud to other members of their class. It is not necessary to discuss the sentences at this point with the class.

Group Activity: Allow class members to offer helpful suggestions for the situations read aloud by the volunteers.

© 1998, YouthLight, Inc.

Student Responses for Conflict Resolution:

Teachers should incorporate conflict resolution into their curriculum and teach the class appropriate ways of dealing with conflict. The following represent topics to be dealt with in conflict resolution:

1. Building a cooperative community

2. Teaching students appropriate social skills

3. Enabling students to communicate effectively

4. Encouraging students to become helpers

More in-depth strategies on these topics can be found on the pages to follow.

© 1998, YouthLight, Inc.

Building a Cooperative Community

1. Ask the students to introduce themselves to a partner describing their favorite place to go, their favorite food and their favorite ice cream. Ask the partner to introduce the student to the group.

2. Ask each student to complete a short biographical sheet. Play a guessing game with the sheets and see if the students can guess which student each belongs to.

3. Play "Human Bingo." Ask children to circulate the room and obtain signatures on spaces which have unique talents and/or abilities on them.

4. Place a picture of a tree in the room. Hang helpful acts on the tree. Ask the students to take one "apple" a day off the tree and complete the task. The student is asked to then hang the apple back on the tree with their initials on it. At the end of the week, the teacher can see which apple cards have all been completed or who has completed the most apple cards. This person can win an apple. To make the activity more cooperative, any student completing 8 acts could win an apple at the end of the week. (Note: If apples are too expensive, perhaps the student could win apple candy, an apple award, etc.)

5. Establish bragging time at the end of every day. During this time, students are asked to brag on things other students have done for them. The bragging student would get nothing, but the braggee would get some token of appreciation from the teacher.

6. Establish a system to catch the students being good by giving them raffle tickets or coupons for prizes to be given at the end of the week.

7. Establish a mail system in the classroom in which students can write positive notes to each other. Ground rules should be established to encourage students to refrain from negative comments. Students should sign their names to ensure accountability.

8. Talk to students about "grouchy" words and "grinning" words. Put many examples on the board. Encourage students to use as many grinning words as possible throughout the day.

© 1998, YouthLight, Inc.

Teaching Students
Appropriate Social Skills

1. **Balloon story** - Using a balloon, tell a story depicting angry situations. Each time an angry situation is depicted, the balloon should be blown up a little more eventually popping at the end. The story should be retold after teaching the kids alternative choices to each angry situation. This time, the balloon should be deflated after each situation.

2. **Rabbit trick** - Using the rabbit trick, children can be shown how they can use turn around statements to deal with teasing situations.

3. **Clay** - Using clay, children can be shown how other people can chip away at their special feelings they have for themselves. By teaching self talk, the teacher can teach the children how to more appropriately respond to teasing.

4. **Taking charge method** - Teach children a formula for dealing with other children who are bothering them. Children should be encouraged to complete the following 4 steps before seeking adult intervention:
   - Ignore
   - Talk firmly
   - Walk away
   - Get an adult
   - Talk nicely

   Children should be encouraged to complete each step a number of times before seeking adult interventions. Steps do not need to be completed in order. Students can move directly to step 5 if violence is involved. Role play each of these several times.

5. Play social skills games. Play the No Fighting game, Clowning game, etc. (described in this book).

6. Teach children how to negotiate and develop win-win strategies. Place children in groups and give them problems and ask them to come up with win-win solutions. Examples of problems are as follows:
   - John wants to ride bikes. Mark wants to climb trees.
   - There is one candy bar for three people.
   - There are 5 bears trying to decide whether to live in the forest in the mountains or in a cave by the lake.

7. Ask the students to make a comic strip of a child using the above methods and negotiation.

8. Ask the students to make up stories about superheros and describe how they might solve conflicts. (from *Creative Conflict Resolution*, William J. Kreidler)

© 1998, YouthLight, Inc.

9. Teach a procedure for dealing with problems.
   - Train students to be mediators in the classroom.
   - Whenever 2 or more students have a conflict, have them go to a problem solving corner with the mediator.
   - Encourage the mediator to help the students come to a win-win solution.
   - Ask the students to sign a written agreement with the plan on it.

10. Tell the student if they have angry feelings, there are some things they can do that are appropriate. These include:
    - Asking to go to time-out for a while.
    - Writing about the feelings.
    - Talking to the counselor.
    - Talking to the teacher.
    - Playing with clay.
    - Reading a book quietly in the corner.
    - Going to get a drink of water.
    - Going to the restroom.
    - Doing something for the teacher.
    - Spending time with a classroom pet.

11. Teach children the turtle method of relaxation teaching the children to relax by finding a quiet place to gain control of their feelings.

12. Use literature to define conflicts and allow the children to think of alternative methods of solving conflicts.

© 1998, YouthLight, Inc.

Enabling Students to Communicate Effectively

1. Teach problem solving techniques.

   STAR method:
   - S - State the problem.
   - T - Think of alternatives while considering the consequences.
   - A - Act on one of the alternatives.
   - R - Review the success of the plan.

2. Teach students good listening skills by doing activities:

   a. Friendship groups - Ask students to break down into groups and choose a group leader. Each group leader is asked to ask their group a question and find out the answers. The group leader is then asked to report their findings to the large group. The group is asked to listen carefully and remember what other students' responses were. Teams can win points for remembering what other students' responses were to the questions. Several rounds are played.

   The activity is processed by asking the students to determine how they were able to listen and remember others' responses. The teacher may ask for students with similar responses and students with different responses signifying that these differences are O.K.

   b. The teacher can throw out a question like what would you do with $100,000? Before each student can answer, they must repeat the answer given prior to their answers.

   c. Ask students to break down into groups. Ask the students to talk about a particular question. Whenever the teacher calls time, the listening student is to remember the last 3 words of what the talking student said.

   d. One student is asked to go out of the room. Remaining students are given slips of paper signifying non-listening types of behavior. Examples of this might be: read a book, act sleepy, look out the window, etc. The students are instructed to perform these behaviors when the student outside the room comes in and begins talking. After a few minutes, the talking student is asked how they feel in such a situation. The talking student is asked what the class could do to appear to be paying attention. The class is then instructed to do those listening behaviors when the person is talking. The class could compare the two.

3. Teach the class cooperative games to play. These games are taken from *Cowstails and Cobras* (Kendall/Hunt Publishing, 1984) and *Silver Bullets* (Kendall/Hunt Publishing, 1989), both by Karl Rohkue. Some modifications have been made.

© 1998, YouthLight, Inc.

Word Chains - Break down the class into groups of 2 or 3. Ask each student to write down a word. The next student is to make a word using the last letter as the beginning letter of the next word. Play continues to determine how many letters each group can come up with.

Lap Sitting - Ask the class to stand in a circle. Ask each student to turn to the right and take one step towards the inside of the circle. On the count of three, the group is asked to try to sit down.

Control Tower - Ask for two student volunteers. One will be the pilot of a landing plane. The other will be the person in the control tower attempting to land the plane. The pilot has indicated that instruments have failed and the control tower will have to land the plane. Blindfold the pilot and establish an obstacle course in the room. The control tower must verbally lead the pilot through the obstacle course to a safe landing.

Car Game: See following pages

Willows in the Wind: See attached.

Race to a Tie - Have the entire class race to finish in a tie. Everyone wins.

Line Up from the shortest to the tallest without talking.
Line Up chronologically by birthdays without talking.
Nail Activity - Stack several nails on pieces of wood. See example in class.

4. Ask students to have a bug and a wish or a feel and a want. For instance, a student could say, "It bugs me when you call me names. I wish you would stop." Another example might be, "I feel frustrated when you talk that way. I would like for you to stop."

5. Teach students to work cooperatively in groups. Teach them the meaning of consensus. Ask groups a question such as "You are all going to Disney world and can take 10 things as a group. What would these be and why?" Let the groups discuss the question and come to a consensus. Discuss the ways groups came to consensus.

6. Discuss how people can jump to conclusions. Give the following examples and ask the students to jump to a conclusion.
   • Susan is crying. Why?
   • Joey has his head on his desk. Why?
   • John doesn't speak to you in the hall. Why?
   Discuss other reasons why the above behaviors might have occurred. Discuss the importance of not jumping to conclusions with friends. Adapted from *Creative Conflict Resolution*.

7. Find a picture out of a magazine. Cover up all but a little bit of the picture. Ask the students what they think it might be. Show the entire picture. Talk to the students about the importance of looking at the "whole" picture before making a decision. The whole picture often changes your whole perspective. Adapted from *Creative Conflict Resolution*.

© 1998, YouthLight, Inc.

Knots - Each player has one pair of panty hose in one hand. This player should then give another person the end of their panty hose. All other players should give the ends of their panty hose to other group members. Each player will then be holding panty hose in both hands. Players should make sure that the ends of their panty hose are not going to the same person. The group should now have a big panty hose knot. Through problem solving, the group should work together to untangle the knot such that the group has no panty hose going across the middle. The panty hose should stretch out to make a big circle. Note: Players cannot let go of the panty hose at any time.

Balloon Bash - The group must hold hands and keep a balloon up in the air any way they can. If the balloon drops, the leader will then eliminate body parts that can be used to keep the balloon up. For example, the first time the balloon falls, the group loses use of their hands, then their elbows, heads, hips, etc. For group competition, you may want to see how many times the balloon can be kept in the air without falling.

Piranha River - Group sets two arbitrary lines about 20 feet apart. The group stands on one side of the line and is given construction paper. The task is to use the construction paper to get the entire group to the other side. The rules of the game are that any time the paper is dropped to the floor, a hand or a foot must always be on the paper or it will be snatched by a piranha (judge). The group must work together to determine how best this task might be accomplished.

Frantic - Each player blows up a balloon and at the judge's start signal, each balloon is thrown up in the air. The group's job is to keep all balloons from hitting the floor. you may want to time the event to see what the group's best record for air time is. The group may want to try to beat their own time.

Pole Shuffle - Using the 10 foot simulation of a pole I have provided (on table), place this on the floor. Divide your group into two equal teams with one "penalty" judge. Put one group on one end of the pole and the other on the other end. The two groups are then instructed to exchange ends of the pole without touching the ground. The entire procedure is timed with each touch to the ground being assigned a 15 second penalty.

Have you Ever Circle Game - Ask the group to arrange their chairs in a circle so that there is a chair for each participant except for the volunteer person who stands in the center of the circle. The center person then asks a "have you ever . . ." question. If a seated player answers the question "yes," then the person leaves the chair to find an empty one. If they answer "no," that person stays in that chair. The person in the center rarely stays for more than one question because their positioning usually allows them to grab an empty chair. Some questions are:

- Have you ever had five pieces of bubble gum in your mouth at once?
- Have you ever drowned an ant on purpose?
- Have you ever ridden a jet ski?
- Have you ever ran a stop sign at more than 30 mph?
- Have you ever seen more than three theater movies at once?
- Have you ever been rock climbing?

© 1998, YouthLight, Inc.

- Have you ever swallowed a live goldfish?
- Have you ever let your fingernails grow more than an inch?
- Have you ever given yourself a haircut?
- Have you ever been stung by a honey bee, wasp, hornet, red fire ant, black fly, or mosquito?
- Have you ever baked a cake from scratch?
- Have you ever just eaten one potato chip when the whole bag was there?

Medley Relay - This is a relay where the group competes against themselves or against a time or distance they have previously established. Each member of the team must perform his or her best effort toward increasing the team's distance from a starting line. The performances are done in sequence, i.e. one after another with each attempt carefully marked and measured. Some events to include are as follows:

1. Standing broad jump
2. Standing backward jump
3. Cartwheel
4. One-legged hop on each foot
5. Somersault
6. 5 giant steps
7. Running long jump
8. One body length

The Wave - Join with another group-playing with at least 15 people if possible. Sit in a circle with the chairs fairly close together. Ask a person to leave his or her chair empty and stand within the circle of seated bodies. As soon as the person moves toward the empty chair, that chair must be filled by a person sitting next to it which will result in a clockwise movement of people. As one person moves, the next person must be in motion in order to fill the vacating seat. When it gets his or her bottom into the empty chair, the displaced person must immediately look for and pursue the empty chair. No time-outs.

Word Scramble - Leader should get alphabet letters and give several to each group member. One member is the caller. The caller can call words and the group has 20 seconds to form the word. Points can be awarded to the group for forming the words correctly within the allotted time period. May want to start with easy words like dog and move to more difficult words like special. More points could e awarded for longer words. As a surprise, the leader could yell free style and the group members could form whatever word they chose. Time limits may be changed according to the group. Time may need to be shortened to add challenge or lengthened if the group is unable to get any words.

Speed Rabbit - (Better with a larger group) - The group makes a circle with one person in the center. Person in middle points to a person in the circle and yells an animal name. At this time, this person plus the people on the left and right must form an animal. The following three animals may be used:

© 1998, YouthLight, Inc.

1. Elephant - Person pointed to puts both hands together to form a trunk. Person on either side must flap their hands next to the center person's ears to form flapping ears.
2. Rabbit - Person in center hops up and down. Person on both sides stomp their feet.
3. Cow - Person in center interlaces finger of both hands and presses both palms out and away from body with thumbs pointing to ground. Persons on both sides must grab a thumb and mime a milking motion.

You can make up more animals if you like.

Sticky Wicket - Have people line up shoulder to shoulder facing in opposite directions. Using a full roll of masking tape, ask the first person to stick the tape firmly to his or her body at about waist level (all the way around) and pass it on to the next person. The next person is to put the tape around or on them. The entire group should continue until everyone had the tape around them. The group is then given a destination that they must try to reach as an encircled group and without parting the tape.

Electric Fence - Using a small piece of rope or twine, tie the rope to two chairs high enough so it cannot be easily be stepped over. The group's task is to get everyone over the rope without touching the rope. One group member can be the judge. If any group member touches the rope, the entire group must go back across.

Hop as One - Players in a line lift and extend their left leg so the person behind can grab the ankle or heel. They then place the right hand on the right shoulder of the person in front of them. Ask the group to start over if someone falls.

Hula Hoop Pass - The group holds hands and forms a circle. Using a hula hoop (or a simulated hula hoop) the group must put the hula hoop over two arms. The group must then pass the hula hoop around the circle. The group may add another hula hoop going in opposite directions or time itself for fun.

Car Game - Pair up with one other person. The person in front becomes the car. The person behind becomes the driver. The driver places his or her hands on the car's shoulders. The car then closes his/her eyes and the driver tells the car where to go by verbal commands. An obstacle course can be set up or boundaries decided upon. If several cars and drivers are moving around, this actually becomes a bit of an obstacle course. "Driving" continues for a few minutes and then the car and driver can switch places.

Process the activity by talking about the importance of accurate commands in trusting someone. If the drivers had given erroneous commands, difficulties could have arisen. Discuss the importance of honesty in relationships.

Willows in the Wind - Form a circle with group members standing shoulder to shoulder. One person is asked to volunteer and stand in the center of the circle. This person then falls from person to person with group members gently pushing the person around the circle.

© 1998, YouthLight, Inc.

A variation of this activity is to have sets of two group members lock arms (holding onto wrists) and form a line with several pairs. The line should be formed such that a person could fall back on these arms and not fall to the ground. Ask for volunteers to "fall."

This activity may be processed by discussing the importance of trust in relationships. How can trust be formed? Group members had to do what they said they would do. Discuss why honesty is crucial in relationships and why people must be reliable and do what they say they will do.

© 1998, YouthLight, Inc.

"Sunshine" Game

PURPOSE:

To teach children methods of responding to teasing comments from other children.

PROCEDURE:

1. Make 15 to 20 sunshines to place on the floor.

2. Ask two children to participate in the sunshine game show. These children can wear sunshine faces.

3. Ask one student to be a cloud. This student can wear a cloud (a trash bag with a hole in the top).

4. A sand timer is turned over to start the game.

5. Ask the two children to try to step across the sunshine one at a time. Whenever the children step, the student playing the cloud should give them a teasing comment or a put down. The student stepping on sunshines must respond with either a positive I statement, a humorous remark, or some other turnaround statement. Children are not allowed to say put downs in return or comparison remarks, like "I'm smarter than you."

6. The children are awarded points for how many are able to cross before the timer runs out.

7. Discussion is focused on maintaining sunny thoughts even when others may want to make our days cloudy. Explain that through using positive self-talk, one can prevent such thoughts from taking root.

FOLLOW-UP:

The teacher can discuss how to deal with teasing comments and challenge students to try these strategies during the week. Discussions could center around appropriate responses that do not include put downs.

© 1998, YouthLight, Inc.

"Monster" Game

© 1998, YouthLight, Inc.

> ## PURPOSE:
>
> **To teach children to respond to teasing comments of others.**

PROCEDURE:

1. Make a large Monster out of cardboard.

2. Have the children sit in a circle.

3. Ask one children to play the grouchy monster.

4. This grouchy monster's job is to ruin all the children's day by stealing all their special feelings. Children are told that the way to tell if the monster stole their special feelings is to see if he could make them start acting grouchy too. Grouchy children put other children down, have angry looks on their faces and even hit other people sometimes. Grinning children respond to teasing by using turnaround statements and maintaining positive feelings about themselves.

5. The leader should lead the children in a chant to make sure they have enough "special feelings." The chant can be changed every time. Usually the children are asked to hit the floor 2 times and clap their hands 2 times. This will establish the beat. Each time, the children can repeat a different phrase 3 times. Examples of phrases might include: I am smart, I am special, I am terrific, I help others, etc.

6. After the chant is repeated, the monster is asked to sneak in the circle and look for special feelings to steal. The monster will do this by saying a put down statement to one of the children. The children are told the secret of scaring the monster away. They can do this by stating a turnaround statement back to the monster.

7. No put downs are allowed. No comparison statements are allowed. ("At least I'm smarter than you.")

8. After the student does "scare" the monster away, the other children are encouraged to clap for this child.

9. Children can take turns being the monster.

FOLLOW-UP:

Discussion can center around continuing to use these turnaround statements whenever put-downs arise in the classroom.

95

"Clowning Around" Game

PURPOSE:

To help children learn to respond to teasing statements.

PROCEDURE:

1. Make a game board which has about two thirds blank spaces and one third clowning or silly faces spaces. The game board should have a beginning and an end.

2. Make Teasing Comments questions cards. These questions would have teasing comments that other children might make to boys and girls. The clowning or silly faces questions would be silly pantomimes that children could do. Examples might be bark like a dog, act like you're playing the piano, etc.

3. The class should be divided into two teams. Teams will compete by seeing who can reach the end first.

4. Students can win in one of 2 ways. They can either get the number of points on a card and get the most points, or they can win by reaching the end first.

5. If a child lands on a blank spot, they can pick a question to answer. If they land on a silly face, they can pick a silly card and perform the pantomime until it is their teams turn again.

6. Play continues until one team wins.

FOLLOW-UP:

Discussion centers around dealing with teasing comments and responding with appropriate comments. Students are encouraged to continue utilizing these skills in their day to day interactions with other students.

© 1998, YouthLight, Inc.

Encouraging Students to Become Helpers

- Allow students to become peer helpers to younger students.

- Utilize paired learning in the classroom.

- Use mentors from the community.

- Use cooperative learning.

- Allow students to help around the school.

- Organize a free car wash for the students to do for teachers.

- Ask the students to perform a play for younger students.

- Give students jobs to do around the classroom.

- Allow students opportunities to write about ways they have helped people.

- Keep an ongoing list of ways students can help other people.

© 1998, YouthLight, Inc.

Unique Strategies for Dealing with the Angry/Aggressive Student

Most of the following strategies will be useful in dealing with students from upper elementary school to high school. For younger students, teachers should use time-out and redirection as much as possible. Teachers at all levels may have to refer the "angry" student for counseling, conflict resolution, social skills training, and/or extra help outside of school.

Use of "Matter of Fact" Approach

When dealing with the angry student, it is important to remain as calm as possible. The angry student is probably used to hearing parents and others yell and use loud voices. The student probably expects the teacher or adult to get loud with them. By using a calm, level-headed approach, it may actually help the angry student to begin to "cool down." Teachers who use the "passionate" approach of discipline with the angry student may actually be making things worse.

Escape Passes

The angry student needs to begin to control his or her anger and be more responsible for his or her actions. This strategy offers the student a way to avoid getting angry and to escape, temporarily, from the situation that is causing the anger. The student is given a certain number of cardboard/paper passes. When the student begins to get upset, he/she may give the teacher one of the passes. This allows the student to leave the room for a few minutes. The student may sit in the office, go to the library or use the bathroom. Once the student is "under control," he/she returns to class. The passes usually are for only three to five minutes.

Redirection List

The teacher keeps a list of errands at her desk. When she notices a student starting to get angry, she looks at her list of errands and has the student complete the task. Suggestions include: take articles to office, take note to another classroom, check the teacher's mail box, etc.

Manipulatives

Some teachers allow the angry/aggressive student to use manipulatives at their desk. As long as the student is not being too loud or distracting others, he/she may use manipulatives at certain times during class. The best kind of manipulatives are the ones that take a little power or pressure to put together or take apart. This keeps the student's hands busy and it burns off some of his or her "extra" energy.

© 1998, YouthLight, Inc.

Teach Self-Talk

Encourage the angry student to use self-talk. Have the student practice this method. Some teachers actually write affirmations or "self-talks" on a 3" X 5" card and tape it to the student's desk. Statements could include: "I can handle this, it's no big deal," "I'll survive," "Tomorrow will be a better day."

Getting in the Last Word

The angry student always wants to "get in the last word." Some teachers allow this (as long as the last words are not disrespectful) while other teachers are determined that they (the teacher) will "get in the last word." Try this approach; **invite** the angry student to "get in the last word." For example, during a confrontation, say to the student, "I know you wish to get in the last word, so go ahead and say what you wish." By doing this, the student feels he/she has gained some power but really you, the teacher, has the power because you allowed the student to finish. Quite often when you try this approach, you catch the students "off-guard" and they do not know what to say.

Taking a Stand

When dealing with the angry student, it is important not to stand too close to the student . . . this becomes a threat. Also, do not confront the student face-to-face. Stand to the side and talk to the student. This means little eye contact. A face-to-face, eye-to-eye confrontation with an angry student would not be advisable.

Take a Humor Break

One teacher keeps a mask and a funny-sounding horn at his or her desk. When the teacher senses too much stress in the room or if he/she notices a certain student getting angry, the teacher will quickly put on the mask and blow the horn. Students usually start to laugh. The horn means that the teacher tells a funny story, reads a joke, or asks a silly trivia question. This tactic can do much to defuse a tense situation.

Empathic Assertion

This calls for the teacher to make a statement to the angry student in such a way to let the student know that the teacher is aware of the situation and is aware of just exactly what is making the student angry. For example, the teacher might say, "John, I know you are disappointed you didn't make the team after practicing as much as you did," or "Sally, I don't blame you for getting angry, Erin should not have said that." By letting the students know you understand where "they are coming from," you can actually lessen the chances of a major outburst.

Fogging

Fogging is a way of confusing provoking parties by appearing to agree with them. When a student says," You're the meanest teacher I've ever had," respond with, "Thank you for the compliment" or "You're probably right." If a student makes a "not-so-nice" comment about your clothes, say, "You really think I have no taste."

© 1998, YouthLight, Inc.

99

The Pressure Point

This is one method that I have found successful with several students who had difficulty controlling their anger. I trained the students to recognize certain things that caused them to get angry. As soon as they witnessed or heard something that caused them to get angry they were immediately told to press their thumb and middle finger together, firmly, for ten seconds. By delaying ten seconds, the students were able to "calm down," think, and not over-react.

A Call for Help

If you have an angry/aggressive student in your room, you may need to come up with a plan of action to get help when necessary. Seek the assistance of a student in your class. Let Tasha know that when you look at her or call her name and pull on your right ear, she is to go for help as soon as possible.

STP

The STP Theory works well with students in grades 2-5. The famous racecar driver Richard Petty uses STP oil to keep his car "Running Smooth." Students are trained to use their STP when they get upset and are not "running smooth." When a student gets angry, he pretends to take his STP.

     S - Stay Cool
     T - Think
     P - Practice (teacher gives students suggestions for solving problems)

The Two-Minute Warning

Allow the angry student a short period of time to calm down. Don't try to reason with him or her when he/she is very angry. If the student doesn't settle down in two minutes, he/she may be asked to leave the room.

Let's Make a Deal

Many angry students show improvement through the use of written contracts. The contracts need to be short term and positive. The student can earn special privileges for controlling his anger.

Everybody Needs an Ally

Let the student know that you wish to help her . . . you're not her enemy, you're her ally. Offer to listen/talk with her after class. Suggest professionals, churches, classified staff and others who are willing to help. Find out what interests the student has. It is amazing what a pack of basketball cards or a poster can do to build a promising relationship.

© 1998, YouthLight, Inc.

Suggestions for Handling Hostility in Students

Look for the Antecedent

Hostile behavior is usually quite predictable in that there is usually an antecedent to indicate future acting out behavior. An antecedent may be a change in the student's behavior or it may be the beginning of a "bad mood" for the student. It may begin with the student yelling out or dropping a book. An appropriate response might be to tell the student that you realize they are upset and that you would like to talk with them after you have started the class in an activity. At this time, you can talk to the student outside the classroom and make a plan for the student to deal with the hostile feelings before they become more explosive.

Use Verbal Decoding

Instead of assuming every action is against you as the teacher or counselor, use reflective listening to get at the underlying message. For example, if a student drops their books, the teacher might respond, "It looks like you're upset today."

Be Direct and Succinct

Moralizing, lecturing, and long rationalizations will not "sink" in to a student who is extremely angry. Short, succinct sentences or commands work best.

Use the Student's Name

If a student is upset, they may not be acting and behaving as they normally would. To use a student's name over and over, has a way of calling the student back to who they are.

Back Away From the Student

Most teachers tend to approach students when they are angry. This may appear threatening. Take a few steps back and hold your hands to the side. This is a universal peace sign and is much less threatening.

Do Not Appear Frightened of Student's Anger

If teachers appear frightened, scared or anxious, students will know they are in control. Always send the message that the school and you are in control.

Do Not Tolerate Any Signs of Graffiti in the School

Paint, wash over, and get rid of anything obscene or suggestive of student or gang power in the school. This establishes the mood of who's in charge. Don't let it be the kids.

© 1998, YouthLight, Inc.

Have a School Plan

All teachers need to know what to do in case of a fight. Several teachers should always respond. One should remove the rest of the class. One should remove dangerous objects. One or two should try to calm down the fight by the least restrictive methods first. Some teachers should know therapeutic holds for restraining students if necessary.

Use the Student Councils

Most students do not like fighting either. Involve the school in coming up with a plan to deal with disruptive students.

Maintain Structured Rules

Aggression occurs less in structured environments. Permissive environments tend to encourage hostile behavior.

You're Right

To deserved criticism, responding with "you're right" serves to prevent the conflict from going any further. To undeserved criticism, saying "you're right" but adding the excuse. It is also important to follow these statements with appropriate plans to correct the action.

Have Dress Codes

If gangs or weapons are problems, establish dress codes to prevent gang paraphernalia from becoming too obvious in the school.

Invite the Students to Talk With You

Sometimes merely taking time to talk with the student will go a long way towards solving any problem.

Have a Fight Form

Develop a form that has particular sections for information on it that must be completed by students. The form must have several primary components including the following: statement of the problem, contributing factors to the problem, how students intend to alleviate the problem and signatures.

Watch the Atmosphere You Create in the Classroom

Competition increases conflict. Allowing cliques to develop increases conflict. Encouraging children to win at all costs encourages conflict. Allowing a non-supportive atmosphere encourages conflict. Frustrating a student by placing unreasonably high demands on students encourages conflict. Labeling some students as "bad" before they are given a chance can encourage conflict. Expecting students not to get along encourages conflict.

© 1998, YouthLight, Inc.

Have a Fight Plan

Break up the fight. Get help if the kids are too intense or bigger than you. Don't expect or demand that the kids talk right away. Give them a place to have a time out either inside or outside of your room. Work out a plan when children are calmed down.

Methods of Working It Out

- Mediating - Each child can tell their side and both can suggest solutions.
- Fight form - See description
- Teach the children to be assertive.
- Use I statements.
- Use a calm voice.
- Watch body language.
- Use behavior contracts.
- Use non-verbal cues.
- Use problem solving techniques.
- Use classroom meetings.
- Use group incentives.

Plans for Dealing with the Extreme Hostile Student

1. Reward other children for ignoring the child who is having the tantrum. Reward the "hostile" child for each period of time he/she does not have a tantrum. This can be done with a behavior contract. Whenever the "hostile" child has reached a certain number of stars of points, have a class reward or party. If giving out treats, allow the hostile student to pass them out. (Social reinforcements and peer pressure help to reduce the tantrums.)

2. Give a time out for the child with the tantrum. For every 90 minutes of tantrum free behavior, give the class a treat allowing the "hostile" student to pass out the treat.

    Greenberg, D.J. and O'Donnell, W.J. "*A note on the Effects of Group and Individual Contingencies upon Deviant Classroom Behavior.*" Journal of Child Psychology and Psychiatry, 1972, 13, 55-58.

3. Allow an opportunity for the child to release pent-up energy. Jogging for 10 minutes may reduce aggression by up to 50% with the maximum benefit being after the first hour.

    Allen, J.I. "*Jogging Can Modify Disruptive Behaviors.*" Teaching Exceptional Children, 1980, 12, 66-70.

© 1998, YouthLight, Inc.

Sherman Tanks

"Sherman Tanks" are students who display their attack weapons and armor clearly for all to see. They are openly hostile and the quicker people realize this, the better for them, according to the student.

Characteristics:

1. These students may be openly:
   - abusive
   - abrupt
   - intimidating
   - overwhelming
   - arbitrary
   - arrogant
   - assaultive
   - critical
   - argumentative
   - antagonistic

2. These students may refuse to display much impulse control, choosing to ignore the rights of others.

3. These students may gain power through their abilities to arouse confusion, fear, and hurt in others.

Underlying Causes:

1. These students may be holding a lot of inner pain and are unconsciously attempting to resolve and heal their wounds by striking out at others.

2. These students may respond aggressively due to poor impulse control when a need is not met.

3. These students may be experiencing violence or neglect in their families. Insensitive acts and violent outbursts may be the only coping skills modeled for these children in their homes.

4. The media, as well as some rock groups, "glamorize" violence as well as "normalize" violence as a means of dealing with problems. (See the following section, "Television Violence.")

5. Alcohol and drug usage lowers ego control and induces impulsivity.

6. Many boys tend to believe that violence is the earmark of their masculinity and somehow "proves" something. Current gang activity supports this theory.

7. Lacks discipline and hostile attitudes from parents, may lead to poorly controlled children.

© 1998, YouthLight, Inc.

8. Children may respond angrily to loss or grief.

9. Children may need to prove to themselves and others that their view is right.

10. The hostile student's view of his or her world is absolute - clear and concrete, straight forward and simple.

11. These students think more in terms of "shoulds" and "musts" instead of "cans" and "wills."

12. These students lack empathy and trust that causes overuse of aggression.

13. These students may demean others to create sense of self-importance and superiority. "If I can make you out to be weak, faltering, or equivocal, then I will seem, to myself and others, strong and sure.

Strategies:

1. Teach social skills or appropriate ways to deal with anger.

2. Limit exposure to TV and rock group violence.

3. Encourage parents to try to work out differences in amiable ways.

4. Encourage parents to provide consistent limits and consequences for negative behavior.

5. Children should be encouraged to explore and discuss negative feelings .

6. Reward desired behaviors.

7. Ignore as much as possible unless the behavior poses a physical threat to the safety of another.

8. Teach assertive responses.

9. Teach problem solving or conflict resolution skills.

10. Help children learn self-control by learning to relax, count to ten, or use self-talk.

11. Provide consequences for negative behavior.
   • Time-out is good
   • Take away privileges
   • Make restitution to the injured party. If the child is young and a blow was rendered, one may ask the child to pat the injured area for a while.
   • Physical punishment would probably be counter-productive.

12. Offer more positive male models who handle aggression in a positive manner.

© 1998, YouthLight, Inc.

13. Foster feelings of empathy.

14. Make sure you look for underlying causes.

15. Do not fill "Sherman Tanks'" expectations by exhibiting fear or rage or be put out of commission. Avoid open confrontation.

16. Stand up for yourself. Use the Broken Record and/or Fogging Technique(s).

17. Give them time to relax. Breathe deeply and "center" yourself. Look directly at the yeller.

18. Don't worry about being polite, just get into the conversation. Be factual and calm. "You interrupted me." Smile.

19. Get attention carefully. Use the person's name; do something unexpected - drop a book. Be cautious of body space; don't look like you are going to attack.

20. Get the student to sit down. "If you are going to argue, we might as well be comfortable." Maintain eye contact.

21. Speak from your own point of view. Use phrases: "In my opinion . . . ," "I disagree with you." Paraphrase and summarize.

22. Avoid a "head on" fight or power struggle. You may lose the battle. If you win a fight, you may win the battle but lose the war!

23. Be ready to be friendly. "Stand up" to the bully and he'll be your friend.

24. Have a "cool down" time.

25. Use "diffusing" by focusing for a while on just the facts through summarizations and open ended questions.

26. Use "yielding" in which you refuse to "push back" at the student when provoked. Instead, encourage the student to use words to "let it out" while you listen. This may need to be at a planned location and time.

27. Sit down.

28. Be a good listener to the child's feelings.

29. Do something surprising such as offer something to drink.

30. Remain calm and state that you cannot talk at the present time.

© 1998, YouthLight, Inc.

31. Leave the scene.

32. Consider settling differences through "arm-wrestling."

33. Use films, books, puppets and drama to promote objective thinking about fighting.

34. Prevent fights by establishing ground rules such as, "when two students are fighting, the students watching will remain silent."

35. Redirect the hostility by combining a reprimand with a dignified command.

36. Conduct a small group meeting of four to six students to confront and listen to the "Sherman Tank." Make sure to pinpoint and include a discussion of his or her feelings, too.

© 1998, YouthLight, Inc.

Television Violence

By the age of two or three, most children regularly watch
26-33 hours of television each week.

Of all households, 98% have at least one TV turned on
an average of 6 hours per day.

In an average evening of television viewing, deadly weapons
appear about nine times per hour.

Of all prime-time network dramas, 75% contain some
act of physical, mental, or verbal violence.

40 percent of all prime-time TV shows are considered
to be very high in violence.

The average child has watched the violent destruction of
more than 13,000 persons on TV by the time he/she is fifteen.

At current rates, the average American will view 45,000 murders
or attempted murders on television by the age of 21.

The typical American child sees on television
75,000 incidents of drinking by the age of 21.

Of parents, 78% have used the television as a
"baby sitter" at one time or another.

By the time of high school graduation, most children
will have spent 11,000 hours in school, but more than
22,000 hours in front of the TV.

© 1998, YouthLight, Inc.

Robie, Joan Hake. *Turmoil in the Toy Box II.*

"Non-Violent Alternatives to Fighting"

> ## PURPOSE:
>
> **To teach nonviolent alternatives to dealing with hostile attacks from other children.**

PROCEDURE:

1. Make a spinner by cutting a circle out of poster board with a brad attached to the center.

2. Copy or rewrite the following alternatives on the edges of the spinner:

Walk away

Use humor   Do something fun

Try talking   Exercise

Change your seat   Relax your body

Take some time

3. Ask each child to draw a picture or write about something that makes them very angry.

4. Allow the children to take turns drawing a card and spinning the spinner. Each child is then asked to describe how the alternative that he/she landed on could be used to solve that problem.

VARIATIONS:

Use the activity in a learning center, small group, or with the entire class.

Divide the class into small teams and have each team earn points for appropriate answers.

FOLLOW-UP:

Discuss what anger really is (it is an emotion that you can feel in your body).

Have students make paper "anger thermometers" that can show how angry they are at any given time.

Have students draw large bugs and write in each "things that bug me."

© 1998, YouthLight, Inc.

"Anger Pictures"

PURPOSE:

To raise children's awareness of alternatives and consequences of actions taken during moments of anger.

To help children learn different ways of coping and dealing with anger.

To teach decision-making and problem-solving skills.

PROCEDURE:

1. Ask each child to divide a piece of paper into four equal sections (either with drawn lines, or by cutting to form a booklet).

2. Ask the children to draw each of the following on one of the paper sections.

   A. Draw a time when you were very angry and did something that hurt someone.

   B. Draw the person after they were hurt.

   C. Draw something that you could have done better, so that no one would have been hurt.

   D. Draw what would have probably happened after you did that.

FOLLOW UP:

Ask students to discuss their responses with other students and brainstorm other possibilities for part "C."

© 1998, YouthLight, Inc.

Snipers

"Snipers" are students who may hide their attack weapons and armor. They carefully look for, or set up attack opportunities. Then they patiently lie camouflaged, waiting for the attack. These students may also be very adept at setting "traps" for others to get caught in.

Like rocks hidden in snowballs, they come at you softly, but hit you hard. They may sound like innuendoes, subtle remarks, digs, non-playing teasing. The victim feels pinned down as if there are no response choices at all. he/she is hit by well-placed verbal missiles, high-powered enough to hurt.

Characteristics:

1. These students are passive aggressive and display hostility covertly.

2. These students may talk behind a student's back with a smile.

3. These students may display incongruencies between verbal and nonverbal messages such as:
   - smiling and rolling the eyes for other students to see when the teacher, or another student does something well.
   - showing a "thumb down" or other negative gesture when someone else in the classroom does something well.

4. These students may provide subtle verbal put-downs.

5. These students may give "hook" compliments.

6. These students may be more effective than "Sherman Tanks" in striking out or hurting others because they are more subtle.

7. These students have developed more skills than "Sherman Tanks" for striking out at others, so that they maintain more control of the situation.

Underlying Causes:

1. Like "Sherman Tanks" these students have firm, self-centered views of how others should behave so that the "Sniper's" needs are met.

2. These students may have deep feelings of hurt, frustration, and/or anger.

© 1998, YouthLight, Inc.

3. These students may need to strike out at others, and have learned that subtle aggression keeps them safer than blatant hostility.

4. These students like to win, and will work very hard not to lose. They like to be in control of a situation.

5. Like "Sherman Tanks," these students may be holding a lot of inner pain and are unconsciously attempting to resolve and heal their wounds by striking out at others.

Strategies:

1. Teach children to use positive self-talk.

2. Encourage children to look at themselves in positive ways:
   -"I Can" Books   -"I'm Special"
   -"I'm Somebody"   -"All About Me" collage

3. Teach affirming activities:
   -"Balloon Game"   -"Batman Cape"
   -"Mailbox Game"

4. Use strength bombardment activities.

5. Help the child focus on accomplishments rather than failures.

6. Involve students in collaborative assessment and evaluation procedures.

7. Teach students the "Superman Shield" as a coping skill.

8. Teach children how to use "comebacks" when they are "cut-down":
   - Ask the "Sniper" what he/she meant by his or her comment.
   - Be tactful and up-front.
   - Say what you think the "Sniper's" words mean, and then ask if you are right or wrong.
   - When the sniper makes negative comments in the group, seek group confirmation or denial of the criticism.
   - Consider underlying causes of the "Sniper's" comment.
   - If there is group consensus that a problem exists, set up regular problem-solving strategies.

9. Teach children how to look, listen, and reach out for allies (peers and/or adults).

10. If you are a third party to the "Sniping," stay out of the middle but insist that it stop in front of you.

11. Take some "think" time.

12. Plan a time to talk about it. Say, "I really need to talk with you. Is there a time to talk? I really need to get my thoughts together."

© 1998, YouthLight, Inc.

Helpful Hints for
Dealing with "Snipers"

---

1. Call the name-caller and his target together for a report of the experience. ("I'd like to have you fill me in on this name-calling episode. Since my memory is sometimes rather faulty, I hope you don't mind if I use the tape recorder." The playback can be very sobering.)

2. Hold a class meeting for the express purpose of discussing name-calling.

3. Hold a joint conference (aggressors and victims) to thrash out differences by drawing up a minimal, mutually agreeable plan: "You've now all agreed to hold the name-calling down to a minimum. John will report to Mr. Jones after recess on the progress of the gang; Jim will report to Mr. Hurley on his feelings. You say you want to try this for a week and you're willing to sign this contract."

4. Ignore the matter, at least for the time being.

5. Meet privately with the aggressor and state directly that name-calling is an act of aggression that is saying "Help!" Then proceed to elicit the student's fears and the reason that he/she feels compelled to lash out against the victim. ("Jenny, you're a bright girl. I don't have to tell you that calling others names is your way of crying for help. What's bugging you so much that you have to do it?")

© 1998, YouthLight, Inc.

"Chip Away"

PURPOSE:

To help students learn that "put downs" can tear your self-confidence apart if you allow them to.

To demonstrate that visual, auditory, and kinesthetic reframing can help one keep his or her self-confidence intact.

PROCEDURE:

1. Tell the story of Mary.
2. Use clay to represent Mary's person.
3. As you tell the story, tear off a piece of clay for each put-down and re-attach the piece as Mary's self-confidence is rebuilt.

Story:

Mary arrived at school feeling great! Today is the fourth grade science fair and she has a great project. She also has on a new dress that her mother bought for her yesterday. She loves it - it is her favorite color of blue. As Mary was putting her book bag away, her friend , Marci, said, " Mary, that is a beautiful dress, even if you did get it at K-Mart." Mary felt her heart beat fast as a piece of her "self" felt broken.

Later in the day, Mary was thinking about some rhyming words that would fit in the poem she was writing for Mrs. von Keller's "Southern Tea and Poetry Hour," an annual event where parents are invited to the fourth grade language arts class to hear the award-winning fourth grade poets and have tea and petit-fours. Her teacher thought she was day-dreaming as she said, "Mary, even though you are looking out the window, I know you must be listening." Mary felt another piece of her "self" being pulled apart.

That afternoon the science fair was the high point of the day - especially since she had been chosen to present her project. As she explained her project to the judges, Ed, a bully in the class - said in a laughing way, "Some science project that is!" as he pointed thumbs down. Another piece of her "self" felt torn.

As Mary prepared to go home, she felt very low - very pulled apart. Then she realized that she couldn't allow put-downs - words - break her. She took a deep breath and closed her eyes. She saw a picture of herself in her lovely blue dress. She knew it was lovely because it was a Jaclyn Smith dress and the color made her look special.

© 1998, YouthLight, Inc.

She thought to herself as she read the poem she had written earlier in the day. The words rhymed perfectly - it was going to be great! As she walked out of the school, she stopped by the cafeteria and touched the Blue Ribbon on her project. She felt so proud!

FOLLOW UP:
- Ask students do explain how Marci was like a "Sniper."
- Have students discuss Mary's changing approach as she received the attacks from the "Sniper."

© 1998, YouthLight, Inc.

"Home Run City"

PURPOSE:

To teach problem solving, appropriate ways of dealing with peer problems, social skills and decision making skills specifically useful in dealing with put-downs or snipe attacks.

PROCEDURE:

1. Divide the class into two teams.

2. Draw a baseball diamond on a piece of tagboard and put magnets on the bases.

3. Draw several "men" and "women" ballplayers. Laminate them and put magnets on the back of the figures.

4. Make up several cards with various problems on them.
   Examples:
   - "You think you're cute."
   - "Wow, what a figure you have!"
   - "You think you have a beard!"
   - "Look at that rat's tail!"
   - "You have a beautiful face except for your nose."

5. Allow the first team to draw a situational card. The team can read the card and choose a "man" or "woman." The person reading the card can then choose 4 people to move the "man" or woman" around the bases. Each person must think of an alternative for handling the problem.

6. If the team can think of 4 alternatives to the problem they are awarded one point or one run for their team.

7. Each team may have 9 "innings" or chances to answer questions.

FOLLOW UP:
Discuss options for dealing with assertive, aggressive, and or passive response.

© 1998, YouthLight, Inc.

Exploders

Characteristics:

- -hostility
- -fighting
- -personal injury to another(physically or psychologically)
- -hitting
- -biting
- -kicking
- -throwing objects
- -pushing
- -spitting
- -name-calling
- -teasing
- -profanity
- -pushing
- -temper tantrums
- -impulsive
- -irritable

Underlying Causes:

1. Temper tantrums are designed to manipulate adults into submitting to a child's demands.

2. Children may learn aggressive behavior as a result of modeling by significant adults or older siblings.

3. Children may be angry as a result of severe emotional upheaval such as abuse, divorce, death, etc.

4. Children may be angry and act out resulting from a psychological need for power.

5. Children may be overtly rewarded for aggressive acts by parents or others who require children to "take up" for themselves.

6. Children may be frustrated by tasks they are required to perform.

7. Children have watched violence on TV programs and hence "model" after their "heroes."

© 1998, YouthLight, Inc.

117

8. Children may be exposed to violence in their culture and grow to imitate it.

9. Music often speaks of destruction and disrespect and children may model it.

10. Students and/or others in their families may abuse alcohol or drugs which may lower inhibitions and increase outbursts.

Strategies:

1. Utilize students' potential for leadership, assertiveness, and independent thinking by teaching them to use personal power appropriately and make effective decisions.

2. Avoid and defuse direct confrontations.

3. Grant students legitimate power.

4. Parents should maintain fun and loving discipline setting consistent limits.

5. Exposure to violence should be limited by parents.

6. Marital strife should be minimized by parents taking appropriate steps to deal with conflict.

7. Children should be encouraged to pursue interests that make them "happy."

8. Teach appropriate social skills and alternatives for dealing with difficulties.

9. Reward desired behaviors through use of behavioral contracts and/or verbal praise.

10. Teach assertiveness in such a way that students can learn to take care of personal needs while coping with others.

11. Discuss actions and consequences on TV.

12. Provide consequences for continued acts of aggression.

13. Utilize "time out" procedures for children to teach appropriate self control.

14. Provide appropriate male role models for boys who obtain "power" in nonviolent ways.

15. Help children learn to understand the concept of empathy.

16. Teach students how to discuss their feelings when they are hurt or angry.

17. Teach negotiation skills.

© 1998, YouthLight, Inc.

18. Show serious intentions, "I can see this is very important to you, but I cannot accept that you . . ."(tell specifically what the child said or did).

19. Suggest that parents:
    • Give each child special time (Research shows that 20 minutes of attention per day drastically reduces whining and aggressive behavior). Use activities chosen by the child.
    • Ignore undesirable behavior unless the act is hurtful to self or others. Offer choices to the child for alternative acts.

20. Provide logical and natural consequences such as:
    • Loss or delay
      - of privileges
      - of participation in an activity
      - of using objects or equipment
    • Loss of freedom of interaction
      - denied interaction with other students
      - required interactions with school personnel
      - required interactions with parents
      - required interactions with police
    • Restitution
      - repair of objects
      - replacement of objects

21. Use the five steps for deflating your own anger.
    • Step One: Acknowledge your feelings.
    • Step Two: Never act impulsively.
    • Step Three: Gain control.
    • Step Four: Explore options.
    • Step Five: Respond in a reasonable manner.

22. Use activities to help children deflate their anger.
    • Therapeutic stories
    • Balloon story
    • Role play
    • Draw a picture of something that makes you mad.
      - Draw two options of something you could do.
      - Draw a picture of you doing the option.
    • Make an anger plan and stick to it.
    • Clay
    • Dramatic play
    • Teach stress management
    • Have each student make his or her own "Anger Booklet."
      Topics include:
      - Think of someone on TV who gets angry.
      - Draw a picture of what they do when they're angry.

© 1998, YouthLight, Inc.

- Draw a picture of someone else you know who gets angry. Draw what they do.
- Sometimes we might get in trouble for what we do when we get angry. Draw a picture of what gets us in trouble for our angry feelings.
- Draw 3 things you can do that won't cause you trouble when you are angry.
- Draw a picture of your friend trying to get you to fight.
- Draw a picture of the way you feel when you're not in trouble.

23. Use the "Feedback Model" (Wittmer & Myrick, 1990)
    Step One: State the specific behavior (action) that bugs you.
    Step Two: Say how it makes you feel (angry).
    Step Three: Say what you wish (want) the person to do instead.
    Example: "When you take my pencil without asking (action or behavior) it makes me angry (feeling). Please do not take it until you check with me first (consequence or result)."

Helpful Hints for Dealing with "Exploders"

1. Appeal to the child's ego with a matter-of-fact statement. ("Barbara, nobody enjoys the Barbara that throws tantrums, but everybody enjoys the helpful Barbara.")

2. Apprise the child of what he can expect from tantrums. ("Billy, tantrums are bothersome to everyone. Don't expect to get favors with them.")

3. Discuss with the student harmless ways of having a tantrum. ("The next time you feel a tantrum coming on, you may use the punching bag in the gym.") Solicit other "harmless ways to "throw a tantrum" from the student and his or her peers.

4. Explain to the child, at a time when he is calm, what the consequences will be the next time he has a tantrum. ("Jerry, perhaps this situation will never happen again, but I want you to know what will happen if it does: I will leave you alone until you stop screaming.")

5. Use nonverbal modes of coping, such as signaling the other students to quietly follow you out of the classroom and closing the door behind you.

© 1998, YouthLight, Inc.

"Deflate the Teaser's Balloon"

> ## PURPOSE:
>
> **To help students learn how to let out their anger in an appropriate and timely way, before they "explode."**

PROCEDURE:

1. Show the children a deflated balloon. Explain that this balloon is like a person who is sleeping at night - nice and relaxed.

2. Then say the alarm clock just went off, while you quickly puff a little air into the balloon so that it stands up.

3. Then, tell them that you realize you are almost late for school and blow a little more into the balloon.

4. Next, on your way to school, some older students see you and make fun of you (blow a little more into the balloon.)

5. When you get to school, someone knocks your books out of your hands and your papers fall across the floor (more air into balloon).

6. Next, you remember you have a big test and you forgot to study for it (more air).

7. At lunch, someone spills their milk all over your lunch (more air).

8. Then, after school you find out that someone has been telling lies about you (still more air).

9. Ask, what do you think is about to happen to you? (answer: pop or explode). Then pop the balloon and discuss how this is what can happen if you let enough anger build up inside of you.

10. Next, tell how you need to deflate or deal with little things that bother you as they happen, instead of letting them build up inside you.

11. Pull out another balloon and tell the same story with some additions. This time, have the person in the story take care of his or her feelings as they happen.
    - Alarm clock goes off (inflate)—Take a shower (deflate).
    - Late for school (inflate)—catch the buss and take a deep breath (deflate).
    - Older students teasing you (inflate)—say something funny back to them (deflate).
    - Books knocked down (inflate)—tell a teacher (deflate).

© 1998, YouthLight, Inc.

- Forgotten test (inflate)—explain to the teacher (deflate).
- Milk spilled on lunch (inflate)—ask for a new lunch from cafeteria workers (deflate).
- Someone is telling lies (inflate)—ask some of your friends to tell others the stories are not true (deflate).

FOLLOW UP:

Teach the children the deflate model on the next page.

Have students role play and discuss other situations and brainstorm ways to deflate their anger.

© 1998, YouthLight, Inc.

"DEFLATE" Your Anger

Deflate deserved criticism by saying "you're right."

Explain that you are going to leave if they continue.

Face them with a smile - don't let them see you down.

Laugh or use a little humor.

Answer "put downs" with "come backs."

Talk to yourself - don't believe what they've said.

Ease your way out of the situation.

© 1998, YouthLight, Inc.

"Win/Win" Guidelines
For Conflict Resolution*

Take time for cooling off if needed. Find alternative ways to express anger.

Each person states their feelings and the problem as they see it using
"I messages." No blaming, no name-calling, no interrupting.

Each person states the problem as the *other person* sees it.

Each person says how they themselves are responsible for the problem.

Brainstorm solutions together and choose a solution that
satisfies both - a "Win/Win" solution.

Affirm your partner.

© 1998, YouthLight, Inc.

* From Drew, N., *Peacemaking Skills in the Classroom*

"Killer Statements Hurt"

> ## PURPOSE:
>
> To become aware of the concept of Killer Statements and to be able to identify them in everyday conversations.

> ## TIME:
>
> One session

> ## MATERIALS:
>
> Pencil/paper

PROCEDURE:

1. Conduct a class discussion around the following questions:

   Have you ever worked very hard at something you felt was not understood or appreciated? What was it? What was said or done that made you feel your effort was not appreciated?

   Have you ever wanted to share things - ideas, feelings, something you've written or made - but were afraid to? Were you afraid that people might put you or it down? What kinds of things might they say or do that would put you, your ideas, or your achievement down?

2. Introduce the concept of "killer statements and gestures" to the students. All of us have many feelings, thoughts, and creative behaviors that are killed off by other people's negative comments, physical gestures, etc. Some killer statements that are often used (even by teachers!) are:

   - We don't have time for that now.
   - That's a stupid idea. You know that's impossible.
   - You're really weird!
   - Are you crazy? kidding me? serious?
   - Only girls/boys do that!
   - Wow, he's strange, man, really strange!
   - That stuff is for sissies.

3. Tell the students that they're going to be social science researchers for the next 24 hours. Ask them to keep a record of all of the killer statements they hear in school, at lunch, at home, and at play. Discuss the findings with them the next time the group meets.

© 1998, YouthLight, Inc.

© 1998, YouthLight, Inc.

Apathetic Students
"Unmotivated Students" & "Daydreamers"

These students, unfortunately, are sometimes labeled "lazy." But, there are always reasons behind apathy in children, and discovering these reasons can open new possibilities in helping them to spark an interest in learning. Apathetic students see little or no personal meaning in their school work and are viewed by their teachers as uninterested, discouraged, and/or distracted.

Estimates of underachievement have ranged from 15% - 45% of all children with 75% being boys (Bruns, 1992). These students can be from disadvantaged homes, but many have parents who are highly educated. Many have average, or above average achievement test scores.

Displaying apathy can be a controlling mechanism which allows the child to dominate the time of the teacher or parent. It encourages the adults to feel guilty that they aren't there enough for the child. It also perpetuates dependency in the child and a blockage of success experiences.

© 1998, YouthLight, Inc.

Helpful Hints for Dealing with "Apathetic Students"

1. Help the apathetic student regularize his or her jobs so that he/she takes care of things on a schedule instead of trying to do them all at once. (What is best done right after school? Before the evening meal? On Mondays? On Sunday afternoon?)

2. Refrain from bailing the student out of situations that arise due to apathy. If you do, you are enslaving yourself to a problem that holds little promise of going away by itself.

3. State clearly what is expected by you. "You may do_____ after you have finished_____."

Eight Ways to Increase Motivation in the Classroom

1. Make sure each student succeeds every day.

2. Emphasize what the children are learning rather than their performance.

3. Make lesson presentations interesting and relevant.

4. Link learning to student's interests. State objectives. Tell students how this applies to their lives.

5. Offer students choices and opportunities for autonomy and creativity.

6. Keep presentations alive by adding variety to routines.

7. Mix learning styles.

8. Find ways students can interact.

© 1998, YouthLight, Inc.

Practical Tips for Motivating Students

1. Utilize counselors, mentors, exceptional teachers to help find "weaknesses" of students. Make a plan with the student emphasizing practical, reachable goals in incremental steps.

2. Find out sources of frustrations. Find peer helpers and mentors to teach students how to achieve success in deficit areas.

3. Allow at-risk students to teach someone else something.

4. Find out what students want to work for and help them attain it.

5. Help students feel comfortable with other people in the classroom.

6. Use cooperative learning and paired learning strategies.

7. Utilize classroom competition with other classrooms through the use of academic games or attained goals.

8. Set reachable goals for the class and offer crazy, or zany rewards for achievement.

9. Have students come up with weekly goals. Make it worth their while to obtain the goal. (Reward, prize, etc.)

10. Have weekly classroom goals. Example: Everyone will bring in their homework this week. We will all make 100 on the spelling test.

11. Try to arrange multiple goals for children. For instance, keeping out of trouble will get a student recess every day, a star on the chart, a chance to go to the 9 weeks trip, a good feeling about oneself, help the class obtain a goal of free time or earn a class trip, etc.

12. Make it worth the class' time to work toward their goals.

13. Maintain a positive, highly responsive classroom environment.

14. Use emotion as a motivator when necessary.

15. Tell constant bragging stories about children.

16. Have weekly awards ceremonies featuring some accomplishment of the student for that week.

© 1998, YouthLight, Inc.

17. Have a hobby day and let students share something they do well.

18. Go after small change.

19. Treat each student with great respect.

20. Encourage students to care about each other.

21. Maximize the individual's contribution to the classroom.

22. Believe that all students can learn.

23. Do not have students always competing against each other.

24. Have a talent show.

25. Show how subjects relate to the real world.

26. Allow students to teach the class.

27. Keep a file of significant achievements that the student has gained. Allow the student to add throughout the year.

28. Give students opportunities to brag on each other every day.

29. Notice when students help each other and make a big deal out of it.

30. Make journals and allow students to write of accomplishments, times they helped others succeed, and notes of progress in academics.

31. Give students pats on the back. (Activity in Gossiping section.)

32. Have school wide incentive systems.

33. Have a student of the week and learn about individual students.

34. Have a parade of excellence.

35. Have a monthly birthday party.

36. Recognize class achievements over the intercom.

37. Make sure students feel "invited" to be at school.

38. Send home cards or positive notes occasionally.

© 1998, YouthLight, Inc.

39. Give students jobs to do around the school.

40. Use students names often.

41. Make sure students get to know each other.

42. Tell students you miss them when they're out.

Motivation
Systems Theory

1. Remember that you are dealing with a whole person.

2. Goals, emotions, and belief systems must be influenced and examined.

3. Realize that a student must have goals if they are to succeed.

4. Realize that multiple goals will strengthen motivation to complete tasks.

5. All goals must be attainable and realistic. They must make sense to the student.

6. Feedback must be given for goals to continue to be maintained.

7. Look for underlying reasons that goals may not be maintained.

8. Look at the environment to see if it is truly responsive to the student.

9. Use emotions as a motivator if necessary.

10. Check out belief systems that may be inhibiting goal attainment.

11. Treat each student with respect.

Adapted from Ford, Martin E. Motivating Humans (1992), Sage Publications.

© 1998, YouthLight, Inc.

Mystery Motivators

The following are several ideas that can be used by teachers to help motivate students. These activities will help students become more excited and motivated. By adding a little "mystery" in the classroom, teachers should see improvement in behavior and academics. Most of these activities can be adapted for use in grades two through high school.

Brown Envelope

On Monday the teacher places a large brown mailing envelope on a wall. A question mark is placed on the outside. Only the teacher knows what reward or treat is mentioned on the inside. Based on the classroom's weekly objectives, those students who earned a reward or treat get to open the envelope to find out what they earned. The reward could be extra playtime, extra computer time, ice cream, homework passes, or a "Pop Corn Party." This activity tends to be successful because the students do not know what they will earn until Friday afternoon. Two or three times a year, the teacher may include a rather big or unusual treat . . . this adds to the excitement.

Caught Being Good with a "New Twist"

Teachers, principals, and other faculty and staff members carry "Caught Being Good" tickets. When they spot a student doing something good or if they feel a student deserves some special recognition, they give that student a ticket. The student must then take the "Caught Being Good" ticket to a special location to redeem (i.e., counselor's office, school secretary, P.E. teacher). The student redeems the ticket by playing a game of chance. he/she gets to throw three dice and add up the points to determine the prize. The prize list is posted and it includes small prizes and at least one big one. A student can win a big prize by throwing "three ones" or "three sixes." Below is a sample prize list for a middle school. A special note here is that recently I used this list at a middle school and during the year only two students won the big prize (cassette tape or CD) but every student who earns a card knows that they have a chance to win a big prize. About 75% of the students will roll a number between 7 and 13 (small prize or a "Sorry.")

Total of Three Dice	Prize/Award
3	Cassette tape or CD
4	Candy bar and a free toss
5	Candy bar
6	Pack of gum or trading cards
7	Pen or pencil
8	Pen or pencil
9	Pen or pencil
10	Sorry (piece of candy)
11	Sorry (piece of candy)
12	Sorry (piece of candy)

© 1998, YouthLight, Inc.

13	Key chain or ruler
14	Key chain or ruler
15	Pack of gum or trading cards
16	Candy bar and a free toss
17	Two candy bars
18	Free pizza or dinner coupon for two

Grab Bag

Place a box or barrel in your class. Have it filled with envelopes or small brown bags. Inside each bag is a small prize. Make sure the barrel includes one "big" prize . . . . this adds to the excitement. Students earning a treat gets to pull out a bag. Prizes may include such things as homework coupons, free ice cream, McDonald's coupons, candy, extra playtime, etc.

The Spinner

Make a large circle board with a spinner attached. Students earning a reward or treat get to "Spin the Spinner" to determine their prize. Make sure your circle board contains at least one big prize.

The Candy Bar Game

Put together a large booklet that contains the wrappers from about thirty of today's most popular candy bars (Crunch, Mars, Milky Way, Twix, Mr. Goodbar, etc.). At the start of a class or at the start of a day, place a candy bar in a brown bag (only the teacher know which candy bar is in the bag). At the end of the class period or at the end of the day, each student who had good behavior gets to guess which candy bar he/she thinks is in the bag. Before the students guess, the teacher shows/reads the Candy Bar Book for the students. The students must guess only the types of candy bars listed in the book. In case of a tie, the teacher flips a coin . . . there can only be one winner. Students must know that they lose their guess if they misbehave. Every day the teacher places a different kind of candy bar in the bag. The winner keeps the candy bar.

How Many in the Jar?

At the start of the week, the teacher places a jar on his or her desk. The jar could be filled with beans or candy. The class decides on a weekly objective (behavior, completing homework). Each day, the students who achieve objective earn a ticket. At the end of the week, each student turns in his or her tickets. Each ticket is worth one guess on "how many items are in the jar." The winner gets the contents of some other prize. The winner is the one whose guess is closest.

Let's Make a Deal

This activity is based on the old TV game show. Every once in a while a teacher may decide to play this game to add even more excitement/challenge. After a student has earned a reward or special privilege, invite him or her to play, "Let's Make a Deal!" If the student agrees to play then he/she must return their prize and select what's behind, "Door No. 1, Door No. 2, or Door No. 3"; the teacher may use envelopes or cards instead of actual doors, or curtains. The student is taking a chance because one of the three choices is bound to be a silly or worthless prize, but one of the three choices is going to be worth more than his or her original prize.

© 1998, YouthLight, Inc.

Trivia

On Monday, give your class a challenging trivia question. The students have until Friday to give you the correct response. A correct response could earn five extra points on a test, free homework pass, etc. Students love trivia questions and will usually work hard to find the answer.

Jeopardy

Students enjoy playing Jeopardy. Teachers can select the categories which can include geography, sports, music, science, etc. Students may have to earn the privilege to play Jeopardy on Friday. To add some fun/mystery to the game, place a star behind one or two of the Jeopardy answers. If a student gives the correct response to that answer then they win a bonus prize.

Wheel of Fortune

On Monday, the teacher places a chart/poster on the wall with a number of missing letters, during the week the teacher will allow certain students to turn the letters or buy a vowel. On Friday the students who earn the privilege will try to guess the phrase. A correct response can earn a prize.

Transition Tickets

Quite often teachers have classes that have difficulties during times of transition (going to lunch, changing classes, etc.). The teacher has a large roll of tickets. Each time the class has to go somewhere, the teacher passes out tickets to those who cooperated. At the end of the week or month, the teacher allows students to redeem the tickets for "mystery" prizes or privileges.

© 1998, YouthLight, Inc.

The Principal's Round Table

Purpose:

The purpose of the Principal's Round table is to randomly select a small number of middle school or high school students to meet with the principal to discuss various school-related issues. The "round table" allows students to get together to meet, talk, and discuss school issues. By randomly selecting students, the principal will have a group composed of students who would generally not talk or meet each other in school. The freshman would be mixed with seniors, males with females, students from different parts of town and county, and students from different cultural or ethnic backgrounds. By mixing groups, students will have the opportunity to meet new people, discuss social problems encountered by their peers, talk about school safety, peer problems, as well as other issues. The goal is that they will gain a better understanding of others and realize that they often share the same concerns. It is hoped that new friendships will be made which will result in a decreased number of conflicts, fights, or disagreements among different cliques or groups.

Method:

1. Each week the principal will randomly select approximately eight students form the school's roster. Each student is notified by receiving an invitation in the form of an attractive card from the principal.

2. The Principal's Round table will meet at the same time each week and the principal and a counselor or a teacher will meet with the selected group for two class periods.

3. All participants will sit in a circle.

4. Some schools choose to name the gathering after the school's mascot. Therefore, instead of being called the Principal's Round table, it could be called the Tiger Round table or the Cougar Round table, etc.

5. Refreshments (usually soda, chips, and/or fruit) will be served.

6. At the end of each session, participating students will receive a button (I was a member of the Cougar Round table) and a cup, water bottle, or T-shirt that displays the school mascot.

7. The principal will serve as a facilitator and will bring a list of discussion topics to help get the group started. The questions could be about the likes/dislikes of high school, current events, school violence, peer issues, etc.

8. The principal will take notes on important topics.

© 1998, YouthLight, Inc.

9. All students who attended at least one round table meeting will be eligible for a drawing to be held at the end of the year to receive prizes supplied by local businesses.

Benefits:

1. Increase in school spirit.

2. Decrease in stress and conflict among different groups of students.

3. Opportunity for students from various backgrounds to meet in a pleasant environment and develop new friendships.

4. Opportunity for students from various backgrounds to see that they often share similar concerns.

5. Opportunity for students to see the principal in a different role and to see that the principal is truly interested in student issues and concerns.

© 1998, YouthLight, Inc.

Unmotivated Students

Characteristics:

These are students who may be excessively:

- disorganized
- forgetful
- dawdling
- not completing assignments
- lonely
- withdrawn
- whining/complaining
- bossy
- aggressive
- hyperactive
- passive
- perfectionist
- dramatic
- socially isolated
- rebellious
- ill

Underlying Causes:

These students may:

1. Have families in which:
   - expectations are too high, or too low
   - parents are overly demanding, or permissive
   - parents are overly neglectful, or protective
   - conflict is intense and/or frequent
   - criticism is frequent
   - sibling rivalry is intense

2. Have a classroom environment that is:
   - not sensitive enough to the student's
     - learning styles
     - learning modalities
     - feelings and beliefs
     - culture and/or ethnicity
     - developmental levels
   - not flexible enough
   - not relevant enough to the student's world
   - not invitational enough socially, emotionally, and/or academically
   - overly demanding, or permissive
   - overprotective
   - overly competitive

© 1998, YouthLight, Inc.

Strategies:

1. Ensure that each of these children is emotionally connected with an adult (e.g., parent or mentor) and a peer who are supportive of the value of the child's schoolwork, and social and emotional welfare.

2. Emphasize that the child is liked for who he/she is, not because of school success.

3. Involve the child in more cooperative learning, team projects, and paired activities rather than individual work.

4. Be supportive and avoid blaming, lecturing, or preaching to the child about schoolwork, but emphasize that it is his or her responsibility.

5. Help these children work with interactive skills and separation anxiety.

6. Encourage parents to be supportive, but not too restrictive with schoolwork times.

7. Be accepting and encouraging. Place a strip of masking tape over the child's desk. Every time the child is paying attention, ask or cue him to make a check mark. Later, send a note home stating how many checks he received. The same thing will work with parents with tape on a refrigerator, or space on a wall in the house.

8. Set realistic goals for the child.

9. Teach and model active learning and problem solving.

10. Reward interest in learning and actual academic achievements.

11. Have a powerful incentive system.

12. Teach effective motivational strategies
    A. Teach self-control
    B. Change the way children look at themselves by:
       • providing feedback rewards.
       • helping child to look at "achievers."
       • changing child's self image to one of success and responsibility.
       • encouraging positive self-talk.

13. Influence school to be more motivational.

14. Do not emphasize or share individual grades.

15. Do not publicly criticize children's poor work.

16. Do not announce that a child who usually does poorly did well.

© 1998, YouthLight, Inc.

17. Do not compare papers or children.

18. Teach children to deal with losing.

19. Involve the student in planning and determining assignments, setting goals, and self-assessment. Encourage student to "PACE" themselves:

P Practice success. Make sure the student has opportunities to succeed many times during the day.

A Actively involve students in planning or determining assignments, setting goals, and self-assessment.

C Change visual, auditory, or affective perceptions of him or herself. Change the method of instruction to use a variety of teaching strategies. Communicate to the child that you value him.

E Encourage students frequently by praise or rewards.

20. Share the following strategies with parents:
- Model positive attitudes toward achievement.
- Don't complain about spouse's overwork or say bad things about the other's career.
- Provide definite limits.
- Give clear, consistent messages toward achievement.
- Avoid giving "yes-no" messages where unpleasant consequences merge with pleasant ones.
- Teach organization and involvement in household chores.
- Avoid nagging.
- Encourage homework study to be quiet, alone and at a desk or table. Do not sit beside child during this time.
- Avoid talking about how you also "hated" school or didn't do well without balancing this with how you "turned things around." This could enhance child identification with parent and encourage underachievement.
- Be aware of own patterns and tendencies toward procrastination, passive, aggressive behavior.
- Maintain power over child in discipline as opposed to child being more powerful or in control of parents and teachers.
- Avoid complaining too much about work - may lead to children complaining about their work/school.
- Parents should resist the temptation to impose their fantasies on your child. Allow them to establish their own goals.
- Beware of equating excessive achievement with happiness.

© 1998, YouthLight, Inc.

People Become Motivated
When Their Basic Needs Are Met . . .

According to William Glasser, "To understand what motivation is, it is necessary first to understand that control theory contends that all human beings are born with five basic needs built into their genetic structure: survival, love, power, fun, and freedom. All of our lives we must attempt to live in a way that will best satisfy one or more of these needs."

Besides survival, our basic needs are:
Love - belonging, friendship, caring, involvement
Power - importance, recognition, skill, competence
Fun - pleasure, enjoyment, learning, laughter
Freedom - choice, independence, liberty, autonomy

Take a few minutes to complete the chart below. Are your basic needs being met in your personal life and in your present occupation or work setting? Are you trying to help your students meet their basic needs in your classroom?

	What are you presently doing in your personal life to meet these basic needs?	Are your basic needs being met in your present work setting? How?	List ways in which you are helping your students meet their needs in your classroom.
Love			
Power			
Fun			
Freedom			

© 1998, YouthLight, Inc.

Highlights of Research on Strategies for Motivating Students to Learn

Research on student motivation to learn indicate promising principles suitable for application in classrooms, summarized here for quick reference.

Essential Preconditions
1. Supportive environment.
2. Appropriate level of challenge/difficulty.
3. Meaningful learning objectives.
4. Moderation/optimal use.

Motivating by Maintaining Success Expectations
5. Program for success.
6. Teach goal setting, performance appraisal, and self-reinforcement.
7. Help students to recognize linkages between effort and outcome.
8. Provide remedial socialization.

Motivating by Supplying Extrinsic Incentives
9. Offer rewards for good (or improved) performance.
10. Structure appropriate competition.
11. Call attention to the instrumental value of academic activities.

Motivating by Capitalizing on Students' Intrinsic Motivation
12. Adapt tasks to students' interests.
13. Include novelty/variety elements.
14. Allow opportunities to make choices or autonomous decisions.
15. Provide opportunities for students to respond actively.
16. Provide immediate feedback to student responses.
17. Allow students to create finished products.
18. Include fantasy or simulation elements.
19. Incorporate game-like features.
20. Include higher-level objectives and divergent questions.
21. Provide opportunities to interact with peers.

Stimulating Student Motivation to Learn
22. Model interest in learning and motivation to learn.
23. Communicate desirable expectations and attributions about students' motivation to learn.
24. Minimize students' performance anxieties during learning activities.
25. Project intensity.
26. Project enthusiasm.
27. Induce task interest or appreciation.
28. Induce curiosity or suspense.

© 1998, YouthLight, Inc.

29. Induce dissonance or cognitive conflict.
30. Make abstract content more personal, concrete, or familiar.
31. Induce students to generate their own motivation to learn.
32. State learning objectives and provide advance organizers.
33. Model task-related thinking and problem solving.

Source: Brophy, 1987: "Synthesis of Research on Strategies for Motivating Students to Learn." Educational Leadership, 45(2). p.45. Copyright 1987 by the Association for Supervision and Curriculum Development.

Underachievement Checklist

CODE: 0=NEVER, 1=SOMETIMES 2=OFTEN, 3=ALWAYS

_____ 1. My child's schoolwork is sloppy and illegible.

_____ 2. My child's projects are often incomplete.

_____ 3. My child procrastinates.

_____ 4. My child is having difficulty keeping up with his or her classwork.

_____ 5. My child's work is not handed in on time.

_____ 6. My child is disorganized at home.

_____ 7. My child is disorganized at school.

_____ 8. My child is irresponsible.

_____ 9. My child is forgetful.

_____ 10. My child lacks pride in his or her work.

_____ 11. My child shows little motivation.

_____ 12. My child avoids academic work.

_____ 13. My child makes excuses for poor performance.

_____ 14. My child avoids challenges.

_____ 15. My child lacks self-confidence.

_____ 16. My child becomes easily discouraged.

_____ 17. My child abandons difficult projects.

_____ 18. My child is easily frustrated.

_____ 19. My child appears to be functioning below his or her potential.

© 1998, YouthLight, Inc.

Interpreting the Checklist

SCORE

0-2 Your child is not manifesting symptoms of underachievement.

3-7 Your child is manifesting subtle symptoms of potential underachievement. His or her school performance should be monitored.

8-20 Your child is manifesting moderate symptoms of underachievement and perhaps a learning problem. This range of scores should be considered a danger signal. Your child's school performance should be very closely monitored.

21-57 Your child is manifesting significant symptoms of either underachievement or a specific learning disability. he/she is at risk academically and emotionally, and active intervention is recommended. You should request that your child be evaluated by the school psychologist.

From: Greene, L.J. *Kids Who Underachieve.* New York: Simon and Schuster, 1986.

© 1998, YouthLight, Inc.

Ten Gifts
That Will Help Children
Feel More Positive About Themselves

Give them *responsibility*.

Give them a *part in decision-making*.

Give them *permission for their feelings*.

Give them *reasonable rules*.

Give them *"guard rails."*

Give them *unconditional hugs*.

Give them *permission to make mistakes*.

Give them *the truth*.

Give them *freedom*.

Give them *themselves*.

Ways To Say, "Good for You!"

I bet your mom and dad would be proud to see the job you did on this.

Thank you for (sitting down, being quiet, getting right to work, etc.)

Thank you for raising your hand, Charles. What is it?

It's a pleasure to teach when you work like this.

I like the way Bill (the class) has settled down.

I'm proud of the way you worked (are working) today.

That looks like it's going to be a great report.

It looks like you put a lot of work into this.

That's an interesting way of looking at it.

Please show it to the class.

This kind of work pleases me very much.

Congratulations! You only missed _____.

Sherri is really going to town.

I like the way you are working.

You really outdid yourself today.

That's right. Good for you.

I like the way Tom is working.

My goodness, how impressive.

You're on the right track now.

Now you've got the hang of it.

That's a very good observation.

That's coming along nicely.

That's quite an improvement.

Everyone's working so hard.

I appreciate your help.

Ann is paying attention.

Now you've figured it out.

That's the right answer.

You make it look easy.

Thank you very much.

Keep up the good work.

That's a good point.

You've got it now.

What neat work.

Excellent work.

Very interesting.

Very creative.

That's clever.

Nice going.

That's great.

© 1998, YouthLight, Inc.

Source: Unknown

Famous People Who
Survived "Difficult Times"
(And Later Achieved Fame Through Excellence)

Louisa May Alcott was told by an editor that she could never write anything that had popular appeal.

Ann Bancroft, a polar explorer, struggled with dyslexia in school, yet in 1986 became the first women to reach the North Pole.

Beethoven's music teacher once said of him, "as a composer he is hopeless."

Admiral Richard E. Byrd had been retired from the Navy as "unfit for service" until he flew over both Poles.

Caruso's music teacher told him, "You can't sing. You have no voice at all."

George Washington Carver was born a slave. When he was an infant, his mother was sold and shipped away. He later held three patents that revolutionized agriculture.

Agatha Christie had a writing disability so severe that she had to dictate her mystery novels for others to type.

Winston Churchill failed the first form (grade) school.

Bill Cosby dropped out of high school. He later received his doctorate in Education and became one of the most successful entertainers and businessmen in the United states.

A newspaper fired **Walt Disney** because he had "no good ideas."

When **Thomas Edison** was a boy, his teachers told him he was too stupid to learn anything. He made 3,000 mistakes on his way to inventing the light bulb. Eventually he held 1,093 patents.

Einstein was four years old before he could speak, and seven before he could read.

The director of the Imperial Opera in Vienna told **Madam Schumann-Heink** that she would never be a singer and advised her to buy a sewing machine.

Michael Jordan was cut from his high school basketball team.

B. B. King lived in poverty as a child and worked in the cotton fields. He become one of the most successful musicians in the history of the blues.

© 1998, YouthLight, Inc.

Abraham Lincoln entered the Black Hawk War as a captain and came out as a private.

Isaac Newton did poorly in grade school.

Louis Pasteur was rated as "mediocre" in chemistry when he attended Royal College.

Wilma Rudolph contracted polio and scarlet fever as a child, and wore leg braces for nine years. She eventually became the first woman from the United States to win three gold medals in track and field in the Olympics.

Leo Tolstoy flunked out of college.

Wernher Von Braun flunked ninth grade algebra.

Fred Waring was once rejected for high school chorus.

Oprah Winfrey suffered sexual abuse in her past, yet she became the first black women to host a nationally syndicated weekday talk show and to own her own television and film production company.

F. W. Woolworth got a job in a dry goods store when he was 21, but his employers would not let him wait on a customer because he "didn't have enough sense."

Summary

What did these people all have in common, in addition to great ability? They took great risks. They took chances again and again. They took their failures in stride and kept on trying. They liked being challenged. They made mistakes and learned from them. You can, too.

"He who never made a mistake never made a discovery."   -**Samuel Smiles**

© 1998, YouthLight, Inc.

(From *Perfectionism* by Elliot & Adderboldt)

"Toilet Paper in the 'I Can'"

PURPOSE:

To help students become aware that they are capable of succeeding at many things.

To help students discover several positive things about each other.

PROCEDURE:

1. Make one or more "I Cans" (A large can coated with pictures of eyes cut from magazines).

2. Divide the class into groups with about four students in each group. Then pass out a roll of toilet paper to one student in each group.

3. Ask that student in each group unroll some toilet paper, tear their section off from the roll, and pass it on to the next student until each has had a turn.

4. After each student has unraveled a section of paper, place an "I Can" in the center of each group. Then, explain that each student is to tear off every segment of their toilet paper. As they tear off each piece, they tell one thing positive (i.e., not hurtful or dangerous to anyone) and place the piece into the "I Can." If a student runs out of ideas of what he/she can do well, others in the group can help him or her.

FOLLOW UP:

When every student in the group has finished, ask them to check to see how many things others can remember about each student.

Have each group discuss how important it is to know what others can do well in the class.

© 1998, YouthLight, Inc.

"Kickoffs For Success"

PURPOSE:
To begin a goal setting process.

TIME:
Two-four sessions

MATERIALS:
Goal setting worksheet

PROCEDURE:

The goal-setting game strategy can be likened to a game of football. The students are team players. The coach (advisor) should review the following information with the class:

Hike
Select one goal! Make sure the goal is reasonable, specific, and attainable in the near future.

Long Pass
Think it and ink it! Write the goal as a specific positive statement. Example: I will spell the days of the week correctly.

Defense
Then write down the action plan. List all the things that can be done to accomplish the goal.

Fumble
Watch out for interferences! Consider all the obstacles that could prevent one from attaining the goal. Example: *There are too many activities in my schedule to allow study time.*

Team
Name the support team. Write down the names of people who can help you reach your goal and list specific ways each person can help. Tell the goal only to the people who can help you achieve it.

Penalty
In the goal-setting game, saying words like, "I can't, I'll never make it," etc., are penalties that set you back and prevent you from reaching your goal. Replace penalty words with positive cheers like "I know I can."

Relay
Draw a picture or write a story about yourself achieving the goal. Be sure the paper includes words that describe how good you feel now that the goal has been achieved.

Touchdown
Put a rock in your pocket to remind you of the goal and every time you touch the rock, think about the picture of yourself winning.

© 1998, YouthLight, Inc.

Goal Setting
Worksheet

---

1. Express your goal in words. Be specific rather than general.

2. When do you plan to have reached this goal?

3. Why did you choose this goal? (What will be gained from having reached it?)

4. Some goals are intangible (like being a happier person). Therefore, they are harder to measure. Tangible goals are easier to measure since they often can be expressed in dollars, hours, people, etc. How are you going to be measuring the progress toward your goal?

5. What are some problems you may encounter as you work towards your goal?

6. What is the first step you can take towards your goal?

   When are you going to take this step?

7. What is the second major step?

   When do you plan to have it completed?

8. List the other steps and anticipated completion dates for each.

IMPORTANT: *Never Give Up*

150

© 1998, YouthLight, Inc.

Other Affirming Activities

Good and Bad Self-Image Pictures

Discuss good and bad self images and what comprises each. Ask children to describe what each "looks" like. After you are relatively sure the children understand, give them each a sheet of paper and divide the paper in half. One half will be entitled good self-image and the other bad self-image. Ask children to cut out two pictures, one representing a good image and the other a bad. Share with the group how a good self-image looks.

Interview

Ask children to interview someone they consider to be successful. Ask this person how they got to where they are, what goals they have, and what they thought of to help them along the way. Present the interview to the group.

Role-Play Puppetry

Teach assertiveness skills using two puppets or two children to act out scenarios. Discuss body rights and teach children to say no when they do not like particular touches. Steps might include saying no, getting away from the situation, and asking a trusted adult for help. Role-play several times to reinforce concepts. Also teach skill (probably in another session) of how to ask for assistance or help when you need to. Again, role-play several times and emphasize those steps that you wish the child to remember.

Batman Cape

Have children attach a piece of paper draped like a batman or superman cape to their backs. All children are given markers and they silently write positive messages to other children without telling the others what they are writing. If possible, allow children to go "trick or treating" for compliments to persons around the school, without "regular" classrooms. At the end of the activity, children take off capes and read them aloud to the group.

© 1998, YouthLight, Inc.

Daydreamers

Daydreaming or fantasizing is important in our lives. Effective decision-making and problem-solving require some dreaming to ensure creativity in the process. Daydreaming can help us to think of new goals for ourselves, and rehearse ways to reach those goals in the safety of our minds.

Daydreaming is also an important part of the psychological healing process. It helps us to consciously begin to deal with grief, loss, fear, and anger. However, daydreaming can become problematic when the intensity, frequency or duration of the behavior begins to interfere with learning.

Characteristics:

These students may be:
- pleasant
- wishful
- imaginative
- escape prone
- creative
- distracted

Underlying Causes:

1. Daydreaming is often an escape from fear, sadness, or anger.

2. Day dreaming may be a critical part of psychological healing.

3. Daydreaming may be a compensation for real disabilities.

4. Daydreaming may be a habit.

5. Daydreaming may help a child feel more powerful.

6. Children may be seeking solutions or a deeper understanding of problems.

7. Daydreaming may be the result of a physical cause such as:
   - brain dysfunction
   - medication
   - illness or allergies
   - lack of sleep
   - substance abuse

Strategies:

1. Plan exciting, busy activities so that the child will have less opportunity to daydream. Real life must become as interesting as daydreaming.

© 1998, YouthLight, Inc.

2. Reward attentiveness and productivity in both tangible and intangible ways.

3. Provide some brief "down times" during the day when it is okay for children to let their minds "wander."

4. Assess the theme of daydreaming.
    Possible themes of daydreamers and activities to deal with.
    A few common themes include:
    *   Divorce
    *   Alcoholism
    *   Physical and/or emotional abuse
    *   Loss
    *   Shyness
    *   Lack of friends
    *   Lack of nurturing at home

5. Write a contract specifying what is expected.

6. Talk with parents.

7. Avoid competition initially as it may cause child to be uninterested.

8. Tap into what the student enjoys doing.

9. Investigate the possibility of drug or alcohol abuse.

10. Help children see the difference between reality and fantasy.

11. Help "Day Dreamers" utilize their imagination to bring about positive self-change.

12. Do not be overly critical, demanding, or abrupt to a child who is daydreaming. Bring the student back to task with a gentle touch, or statement.

© 1998, YouthLight, Inc.

"Beat the Clock"

PURPOSE:

To help daydreamers, or any child who has trouble concentrating, make a game out of any task by challenging the child to try to "beat the clock."

PROCEDURE:

Set a timer for a reasonable amount of time in which to complete the task.

Suggest that the child work to beat the clock, and if they do, they could earn one chip (or other token), lunch with the principal, or to be "Principal for the Day."

FOLLOW UP:

Have students discuss:

- Feelings about "beating the clock."

- The amount and quality of work that they completed.

- Their plans for the next time they work on a task like this. Do they need the same time, more time, or less time?

© 1998, YouthLight, Inc.

"One-Track Mind"

PURPOSE:

To teach children the skill of concentrating.

PROCEDURE:

1. Introduce an activity to a group of children. (e.g. reading books, playing with puzzles, drawing a picture, etc.)

2. Children are told that you will be trying to distract them by talking to them, getting them to stop doing their activity, etc. If they pay attention to you, you are awarded a point. If they do not pay attention to you, they are awarded a point.

FOLLOW UP:

Ask children to discuss the meaning of self-control and concentration.

Ask children to brainstorm the "do's and don'ts" of making sure a person can concentrate in the following situations:

• You taking a test.

• You studying at home.

• Car driver in a race.

• A doctor doing surgery.

• Mountain climber on a cliff.

© 1998, YouthLight, Inc.

"Belonging"

© 1998, YouthLight, Inc.

PURPOSE:

To discuss the feelings of being "included/excluded."

To plan specific actions to include others in activities.

TIME:

One session

MATERIALS:

Green, blue, and yellow dots, pencil, paper (If group is large, another color or two may be added.)

PROCEDURE:

The teacher gives a brief explanation of non-verbal behavior and then explains to the students that a colored dot is going to be placed on the forehead of each person. The colored dot represents a group that they are going to join.

The rules of the game are:
1. No talking!
2. Students must use only non-verbal behavior to discover the color of their dot and to form a group with those who have dots of the same color.

The teacher begins the "no-talking" time and goes around and places the dots on the forehead of each student (without them seeing their color). The teacher selects one student (preferably one who is popular and accepted by others) to get the yellow dot. Then he/she instructs the students to form a group (using non-verbal behavior) with those who have the same color dot.

It will soon become apparent that this one student is not a part of any group. Ask the student to relate his or her feelings about being left out. Then involve the other student to relate his or her feelings about being left out. Then involve the other students in a discussion on "How it feels to be excluded," "What can we do to include others?" "Do new students feel this way?" Discuss the nonverbal behavior that students used to let others know they were included or excluded.

WRAP-UP:

In closing, ask each student to make a special effort during the week to make another person feel included.

Section VII

Special Bonus Section:

Trends in the Home

compiled by:

Tom Carr

© 1998, YouthLight, Inc.

Abuse and Violence
in the Home

- Of 339 cases of physical abuse reported to Iowa's Department of Human Services by non-parents, such as teachers or counselors, 290 were caused by boyfriends. (McManus, 1993)

- "The home is actually a more dangerous place for women than the city streets. Each day, four women are killed by their male partners."

- 99% of kidnappers and the large majority of physical and sexual abusers of children are their parents. (USA TODAY, 5-3-90)

- An estimated 1,200 children die each year from child abuse or neglect; those who survive are often damaged for life. The experience of physical abuse as a child, for example, increases the risk of chronic aggressive behavior by almost 300%. (New York Times, 12-21-90)

- Neglect is the type of child maltreatment most strongly correlated with poverty, incest the least; but economic stress, material deprivation, social isolation, and educational deficits, such as unrealistic expectations of children's capacities - all closely associated with poverty - substantially increase the chance that maltreatment will occur. (Pelton, 1978)

- One study in Wisconsin found that cases of child abuse increased by an average of 123% in counties where the unemployment rate had risen 3.1% or more; counties in which unemployment declined had reduced reports of abuse. (Coontz, 1992)

- 92% of the victims of child sexual abuse are girls; 97% of the abusers are male. Incest tends to occur in families with strong patterns of paternal dominance and authoritarianism, along with values reinforcing the submission of women and children. (Coontz, 1992)

- In a recent survey of 1,000 U.S. adults sponsored by the Family Violence Prevention Fund, found: 14% of the women say they have been beaten by a husband or boyfriend, 34% say they've witnessed domestic violence. (USA TODAY, 4-20-93)

- In this country, a woman is beaten every 18 seconds. Every year, some three million women are smacked, hit, punched, kicked, stomped, scalded, burned, stabbed, shot, mutilated, or sexually tortured by the men who say they love them. Four women a day are killed, many of them after they had left their abusers. (Foley and Nechas, 1993)

- Battered women are seen in emergency rooms more frequently than patients with appendicitis. In one hospital, 70% of the victims of violence are battered women. (Foley and Nechas, 1993)

© 1998, YouthLight, Inc.

- "The most important source of violence by and among children is family breakdown. More that 60% of children born today will spend at least some time in a single-parent household before reaching age 18."

- Researchers at the University of Maryland School of Medicine in Baltimore recently completed a study of 168 teenagers who visited an inner-city clinic for routine medical care. The teens were questioned about their exposure to various kinds of violence. A stunning 24% had witnessed a murder and 72% know someone who had been shot. (Zinsmeister, 1990)

- In a recent newspaper article Arthur Caplan, director of the center for Biomedical Ethics at the University of Minnesota Medical School, noted: The FBI reports that a woman is beaten every 12 seconds in this country. The American Medical Association estimates that nearly a third of the women seen in emergency rooms are victims of domestic violence. The National Council of Juvenile and Family Court Judges says that more than half the men who batter their wives also abuse their children. Government surveys show that domestic violence was responsible for more than 100,000 hospital days, 30,000 emergency room visits, and 40,000 visits to the doctor each year. (Knight-Ridder, 6-24-93)

© 1998, YouthLight, Inc.

Children and Television

- American teenagers spend, on average, about twenty-one hours per week watching television. By contrast, they read for pleasure about 1.8 hours per week and spend 5.6 hours on homework. (Nat'l Center Education Stats. 1990)

- One study found that eleven and twelve-year-old boys watch television an average of twenty-six hours per week. (Timmer, Eccles, O'Brien, 1985)

- Television viewing peaks at around age twelve and declines through later teen years. It may represent the only activity some children share with parents or siblings. (Carnegie Corp. 1992)

- A study commissioned by TV GUIDE reported that in a single day, TV showed 1,846 acts of violence, 389 assaults, 362 gunplay, and 273 punches. (NBC Nightly News, 5-21-93)

- Dr. Branden Centerwell, an epidemiologist at the University of Washington, in a recent study showed that the white homicide rate in the United States increased 93% between the introduction of TV in 1945 and 1974. In South Africa, which had no TV until 1974, it declined 7% during the same period. (USA TODAY, 6-8-93)

- According to Nielson data, by age eighteen, the average American child will have watched 22,000 hours of television. That's double the 11,000 hours spent in school. (McManus, 1993)

- Dr. Brandon Centerwell, an expert on media violence, writes: "TV is a factor in 10,000 homicides each year." (McManus, 1993)

- Dr. Tom Radecki, a psychiatrist who created the National Coalition on Television Violence, says that entertainment violence is responsible for 25-50% of all domestic violence in the United States. He cites studies that show that kids with a heavy TV diet are more likely to solve problems with peers by punching them. Long-term studies show that heavy TV watchers are more likely to become pregnant while unmarried, delinquent as teenagers, and criminal as adults. (McManus, 1993)

- The movie "Robocop 2," starring Arnold Schwarzenegger, has 147 violent acts per hour. (McManus, 1993)

- A study begun on a group of eight-year-olds by Leonard Eron and Rowell Huesmann of the University of Illinois tried to identify all causes of aggression in childhood: child-rearing practices in the family, neighborhood experiences, and other factors. At the end of the ten years, the single best predictor of violence in these children, now 18, was what they had watched on tele-

© 1998, YouthLight, Inc.

160

vision when they were eight years old - not what their families did, not what their social class was, not any of the other things that were measured. (Education Week, 10-4-89)

• Recent research generally identifies three problems connected with TV violence: Children may become less sensitive to the pain and suffering of others; they may be more likely to behave in aggressive or harmful ways toward others. (Education Week, 10-4-89)

• Columnist George Will tells of a study done in a remote Canadian community that first had television in 1973. Before television was introduced, the researchers monitored rates of inappropriate aggression among 45 first and second-graders. After two years of television, the rate of aggression increased 160%, in both boys and girls, and in both those who were aggressive to begin with and those who were not. Other researchers studied third, fourth, and fifth grade boys in two Indian communities in northern Manitoba. One got television in 1973, the other in 1977. The aggressiveness of boys in the first community increased immediately, in the second it increased four years later. (Will, 1993)

• "Next to parents, television is, perhaps, a child's most influential teacher." (Boyer, 1991)

• The amount of time children spend watching television is awesome. A six-month-old, peering through the rails of a crib, views television, on average, about one and a half hours every day. A five year-old watches an hour a day more. By the time the child sets foot in kindergarten, he/she is likely to have spent more than four thousand hours in front of this electronic teacher. (Liebert and Sprafkin, 1988)

• On Saturday morning, during the so-called "children's hour," youngsters are served a steady diet of junk-food commercials and cartoons that contain, on average, twenty-six acts of violence every six minutes. (Radecki, 1991)

• According to a Harvard University study, 70% of today's parents feel that children are watching too much television. Although 40% of parents believe that such viewing has a negative effect on their kids, pediatricians at the University of California found that barely 15% of the parents guide their children in selecting programs. Two-thirds do not frequently discuss program content with their children, and 66 % often use television to entertain. (Taras, 1990)

© 1998, YouthLight, Inc.

Health Issues

- For the past 20 years, government and scholarly estimates of the number of children 18 and under who suffer from mental disorders have hovered around 12% of that population. But a recent report from the Institute of Sciences suggests that figure may actually be as high as 17-22% - 11 million to 14 million children. (The Atlantic, June 1991)

- The suicide rate for white adolescent males has tripled in the past thirty years, as has that of all young people 15-24. (The Atlantic, June 1991)

- "The day-to-day physical nourishment of babies - the quality of care they get during the first months and years of life - will shape profoundly their readiness for school. If there is one right that every child can claim, it is the right to a healthy start." (Boyer, 1991)

- Raising our expectations for educational performance will not produce the needed improvement unless we also reduce the barriers to learning that are represented by poor student health. (Boyer, 1991)

- Mothers who smoke during pregnancy place their child at risk for low birthweight, asthma, and growth retardation. The effects of smoking are cumulative, with children of heavy smokers scoring lower on verbal tests than those of lighter smokers or non-smokers. (Newman and Buka, 1990)

- Approximately forty thousand babies are born each year in this country with serious problems directly related to alcohol abuse by mothers during pregnancy. About 7,000 of them have fetal-alcohol syndrome, a condition that results in mental retardation. Another 33,000 have learning problems, limited attention span, speech and language deficiencies, and hyperactivity. (Newman and Buka, 1990)

- More that 10% of all newborns in the U.S. - 425,000 in 1988 - had mothers who used marijuana, cocaine, crack, heroin, or amphetamines during pregnancy. Cocaine and crack are associated with prematurity, smaller head circumference, and lower birthweight, all of which place a child educationally at risk. (Boyer, 1991)

- In a Carnegie Foundation survey of teachers, more than half of the respondents said that, "poor nourishment" among students is a problem at their school. 60% cited "poor health" as a problem. (Boyer, 1991)

- For every alcoholic, it is estimated that four or five family members and friends, 35-45 million persons, are directly affected by the disease. (Wilson and Blocher, 1990)

© 1998, YouthLight, Inc.

- Children of alcoholics often have school and/or behavior problems, characterized by fighting with peers, temper tantrums, disruptive classroom behavior, poor academic performance, truancy, delinquency, and/or abuse of alcohol and other drugs. (Wilson and Blocher, 1990)

- Children of alcoholics account for some 20% of all referrals to child guidance clinics and approximately 40-90% of case loads in child and family agencies. (Woodside, 1982)

- Eating disorders, which are found most frequently in middle-class female adolescents, have been increasing in prevalence over the past few years. In fact, anorexia nervosa and bulimia are estimated to occur in 5-10% of adolescent girls and young women. (Nassar, Hodges, Ollendick, 1992)

- Data indicate that one out of every six children will lose one parent by death before his or her eighteenth birthday. These losses affect the child's behavior and performance in school. Students often miss classes, do not complete assignments, do poorer quality work, exhibit rebellious behavior, or withdraw into depression. (Glass, 1991)

- The Children's Defense Fund noted the following:
  - In 1989, 20,000 babies were born to mothers who did not receive timely, adequate prenatal care.
  - 10.7 million children younger than 18 (in 1988) were completely uninsured.
  - The poorest children ages 5-17 lose 1.5 times more days of school because of acute or chronic health conditions.
  - Every 64 seconds an infant is born to a teenage mother. Every five minutes an infant is born to a teenage mother who already had a child.
  (Children's Defense Fund, 1991 Report)

- Figures for 1990 show AIDS killed more men ages 25-44 than accidents, homicide, heart disease or cancer in 64 major cities and in the states of New York, New Jersey, California, Florida, and Massachusetts.

- In 1992, 1330 eighth graders in North Carolina were surveyed about their biggest worries, fears, and concerns. Four of their top ten worries had to do with death, dying, and health related issues:

Rank	Worry, Fear, or Concerns
1	Getting good grades
2	Their parents' health
3	Friend, relative, family member dying
4	Taking tests
5	Getting into college
6	Getting a good job after high school/college
7	Not being attractive
8	Dying
9	Going to high school
10	Getting AIDS (Carr, 1992)

© 1998, YouthLight, Inc.

163

- The prevalence for depression in children up to the age of 12, drawn from the general population, ranges from 2% (major depression) to about 15% (moderate depression). (Hopper and Christensen, 1991)

- Prevalence of Attention Deficit Disorder within the U.S. school-age population could conservatively be estimated to be between 3-5%. Boys are four to nine times more likely than girls to have ADD. (Parker, 1992)

- The incidence of learning problems and underachievement within the population of children with ADD was once estimated from 43% to 92%. (Parker, 1992)

- In terms of behavior, ADD children have a greater likelihood than other children of having behavior disorders. It is estimated that between 40 and 60% of children with ADD will show signs of co-existing oppositional defiant disorder (ODD). Half of those children, in turn, will develop a conduct disorder (CD). (Parker, 1992)

© 1998, YouthLight, Inc.

Parenting in the 90's

- In a recent Gallup Poll most modern mothers think they are doing a better job of communicating with their children (though a worse job of house cleaning) than did their own mothers and they put a higher value on spending time with their family than did their mothers.

- In a recent poll, 71% of the respondents said they were "very satisfied" with their own family life, but more than half rated the overall quality of family life as negative; "I'm okay; you're not."

- Many authorities argue that highly aggressive, violent children are more likely to come from punitive, authoritarian families, especially abusive ones, rather than permissive ones. (Coontz, 1992)

- There is evidence that "full-time" housewives are more likely than working mothers to use violence against their children. (Coontz, 1992)

- Sons of working mothers appear to have more respect for women than do other boys and are more likely to see men as warm and expressive. (Coontz, 1992)

- In one study, the families of rapists were far more likely than those of non-rapists to contain wives who were full-time homemakers. (Coontz, 1992)

- "When children are socially and emotionally supported by caring adults, their prospects for learning are wonderfully enhanced. If, however, children are denied this supportive home environment during the first years of life, it will be more difficult for them to succeed fully in school." (Boyer, 1991)

- "The vast numbers of children today grow up in environments that are language poor." (Boyer, 1991)

- According to one survey, parents talk to their children, on average, just a few minutes a day, usually giving orders. (Boyer, 1991)

- A U.S. Department of Education report recently revealed that nearly 30% of today's parents do not regularly read aloud to their children and nearly 60% don't tell their children stories. (Boyer, 1991)

- The arts are an essential part of language which must be developed if school readiness is to be achieved. Yet, according to a recent survey, only 39% of parents regularly engage in music activities with their children. Only one-third engage in arts and craft activities. (Boyer, 1991)

© 1998, YouthLight, Inc.

- The Carnegie Foundation surveyed five thousand fifth and eighth graders. They found that, "60% said they wish they could spend more time with their mothers and fathers. Nearly one-third said their families never sit down to eat a meal together." (Boyer, 1991)

- According to a Louis Harris survey, half of the nation's adults feel that the quality of family life in this country has deteriorated. Three out of four say that problems affecting children today are worse than when they were growing up. 60% confirm that it is difficult to find enough time for their children. (Boyer, 1991)

- A recent survey compared methods of discipline that parents favor today and these methods were compared to those favored by parents 30 years ago.

- Methods of discipline favored by parents: 1962 and 1992:

Type of discipline	1962	1992
Time-out	20%	38%
Lecture them in a nice way	23%	24%
Spanking	59%	19%
Take away TV privileges	38%	15%
Scold (not in a nice way)	17%	15%
"Ground" them	5%	14%
Take away allowance	4%	2%

  *Note: parents could cite more than one method
  (Bruskin-Goldring Research, 1993)

- One survey of 1,000 adolescents found that they spend an average of five minutes a day exclusively with their fathers and about twenty minutes with their mothers. (Csikszentmihalyi and Larson, 1984)

- Eva Margolis and Louis Genevie interviewed 1,100 mothers of all ages and published the results in their books, *The Motherhood Report, How Women Feel About Being Mothers*. Highlights from the study include:
  - Only one in four mothers had very positive feelings about motherhood.
  - One in five views motherhood in a very negative way.
  - Many mothers with children under 12 said infancy was their least favorite stage of motherhood.
  - Twice as many women said their marriages took a turn for the worse after they had children.
    (Foley and Nechas, 1993)

- Attention is important between marriage partners, but it is fundamental for children. Infants who do not get enough attention, in the sense of psychic interaction and love, simply cannot survive, even if they are fed and clothed. In a study in Chicago it was found that the children of "warm families" (families where high levels of attention were given to each member) were significantly different from children of "cool families" (families where parents are distracted and inattentive and did not relate well to each other). Children of warm homes are more sympathetic, helpful, caring, and supporting. Warm homes also breed children who are less denying, defensive, and unsure of their worth. (Csikszentmihalyi, 1981)

© 1998, YouthLight, Inc.

- The book, *New Families, No Families* takes a close look at household chores in the 1990's. Highlights include:
  - Children are helping less around the house than in the past.
  - Educated parents are less likely to require them to help.
  - As a mother's education level rises, the work asked of her children declines.
  - Husbands in highly educated households contribute significantly more than those in less educated families.
  - Women continue to bear the overwhelming burden for keeping the household running.
  - Husbands in highly educated households may be taking up the share of work previously done by children.
  - Husbands are making a greater contribution in households where the mother works more hours and earns more money.
  - There has been a decline in the amount of time spent on housework overall.
  - Women are more aware of the work they do and may not realize all that their husbands are doing, and vice versa.
  - Growing up in a female-headed household results in greater participation in household chores among children than growing up in an intact family, so much that boys in mother-only families are more involved in household tasks than girls in two-parent families.
  (Goldscheider and White, 1991)

  In the book, *Secrets of Strong Families*, the authors headed up research done on 3,000 families. Results from their studies showed that the top six factors that go into the making of a strong family are (in rank order):
  1. Commitment
  2. Appreciation of family members
  3. Communication
  4. Time together
  5. Spiritual wellness
  6. Ability to cope with stress and crisis
  (Stinnitt and Defrain, 1986)

- Therapist John Bradshaw explains away this generation's problems with the dictum that 96% of families are dysfunctional, made that way by the addicted society we live in. (Whitehead, 1993)

- America's young adolescents have a great deal of discretionary time. Much of it is unstructured, unsupervised, and unproductive. Only 60% of adolescents' waking hours are committed to such essentials as school, homework, eating, chores, or paid employment, while fully 40% is discretionary. (Carnegie Report, 1992)

- A recent survey of 25,000 eighth graders found that 27% of the respondents regularly spent two or more hours home alone after school. Eighth graders from families in the lowest socioeconomic group were more likely to report that they are home alone for more than three hours a day. (Carnegie Report, 1992)

© 1998, YouthLight, Inc.

- 70% of women with children under the age of five work full-time. (Brazelton, 1993)

- There has been much research lately on parenting styles (permission, authoritarian, and authoritative/democratic). Time after time, research shows that children reared in authoritative or democratic homes are more likely to be successful in school (better grades and less behavior problems) than children raised in permissive or authoritarian homes. Best estimates are that only 25-30% of homes in the U.S. are authoritative or democratic. (Carr, 1992)

- 152 fourth and fifth graders at an elementary school in Hillsborough, North Carolina were surveyed. The results of the survey revealed that the more successful students had a much more positive perception of their non-school hours. Listed below in rank order are the five areas that the more successful students perceived in a much more favorable way than did the less successful students:
  1. They perceived their families spent much more quality time together.
  2. They believed they had good behavior at home.
  3. They had higher levels of self-esteem.
  4. Their parents were more consistent with following through with stated consequences.
  5. They had no doubts about their parents' love for them.
     (Carr, 1993)

© 1998, YouthLight, Inc.

Marriage and Divorce

- According to polls by George Gallup, what sparked three-fifths of divorces was simply poor communication. (McManus, 1993)

- Half of all newlyweds will divorce. Another tenth will permanently separate. That's a 60% dissolution rate! (McManus, 1993)

- The divorce rate in Europe is half that of the United States. (McManus, 1993)

- Second marriages are just as likely to fail as first marriages. Second marriages that break apart do so more quickly - about six years for a second divorce, after an initial median marriage of eight years. (McManus, 1993)

- About 40% of children will see parents divorce by age eight, and half will see a second pair of parents divorce by age eighteen. (McManus, 1993)

- Research studies show that divorce and the process of marital breakup puts people at a much higher risk for both psychiatric and physical disease, even cancer. (McManus, 1993)

- Research by J.J. Lynch reveals that divorced men are twice as likely to die from heart disease, stroke, hypertension, and cancer as married men in any given year. And death for the divorced is four times more likely via auto accidents and suicide; seven times higher for cirrhosis of the liver and pneumonia; eightfold greater by murder, and psychiatric illness is ten times more likely. (McManus, 1993)

- Larson studied 20,000 white women and found that married women are far less prone to physical illness than are single women who suffer more chronic conditions and spent more days in bed than did married women. For example, divorced women's odds of dying in a given year from cancer of the mouth, digestive organs, lungs, and breast are two to three times that of married women. (McManus, 1993)

- According to the Gallup Poll, only 17% of marriages break up because of adultery. But 47% end because of "incompatibility." (McManus, 1993)

- According to a National Survey of Family Growth sponsored by the National Institute of Child Development, "Those who were active in practicing their faith are more than twice as likely to stay married as the non-religious." (McManus, 1993)

- Psychology Today reported in its July/August 1988 issues about a Swedish study. Yale

© 1998, YouthLight, Inc.

University sociologist Neil Bennett and colleagues found that cohabitating women were 80% more likely to separate or divorce than were women who had not lived with their spouses before marriage. (McManus, 1993)

- The National Survey of Families and Households reported in 1989: "Unions begun by cohabitation are almost twice as likely to dissolve within ten years compared to all first marriages." (McManus, 1993)

- "Have you ever wondered why the divorce rate in Japan is about one-fourth that in the United States? Perhaps one reason is that Japanese choose partners who will be approved by their families, while American couples choose their marriage partners without any regard for family approval. Apparently, the Japanese families have a clearer vision for who is a suitable partner for a child than the adult child has on his own!" (McManus, 1993)

- Of the 1,183,000 U.S. marriages that ended in divorce in 1988, the median length of those that dissolved was seven years. (McManus, 1993)

- Three-fifths of marriages failed due to poor communication, or to poor conflict-resolution skills. (McManus, 1993)

- One Gallup Poll reported in 1989, "In an era of increasingly fragile marriages, a couple's ability to communicate is the single most important contributor to a stable and satisfying marriage." (McManus, 1993)

- Less than one-fifth of all marriages in America were proceeded by marriage preparation courses. (McManus, 1993)

- In a study by Huber and Spitze in 1989, 1,360 husbands and wives were asked, "Has the thought of getting a divorce ever crossed your mind?" They found that more wives than husbands thought about divorce. How much each one earned had no effect on a spouse's thoughts of divorce. Nor did the attitudes about the roles of men and women. But the more housework a wife saw her husband do, the less likely she was to think of divorce. As the researchers noted, "For each of the five daily household tasks which the husband performs at least half the time, the wife is about 3% less likely to have thought of divorce." The five tasks defined as taking the most time in housework were meal preparation, food shopping, childcare, daily housework, and meal cleanup." (Bellah, 1991)

- There is evidence that couples with boys are less likely to divorce than couples with girls. The authors of this study demonstrated this phenomenon and argue that this is the result of the very great likelihood that mothers will get custody of minor children and the greater closeness of fathers to their sons than to their daughters. Hence, fathers with sons are more willing to keep their marriage together at given levels of marital discord than fathers with daughters. (Goldscheider and White, 1991)

- Recent studies estimate that about two out of three first marriages will end in divorce or separation. (Goldscheider and White, 1991)

© 1998, YouthLight, Inc.

- Couples who delay the arrival of the first child at least a period after marriage give themselves time to establish their relationship and their respective roles in the marriage. This reasoning suggests that couples who wait several years before becoming parents stand the best chance of a satisfying and lasting relationship over the long run. (Goldscheider and White, 1991)

- If current trends continue, less that half of all children born today will live continuously with their mother and father throughout childhood. (Goldscheider and White, 1991)

- Half of the single mothers in the U.S. live below the poverty level. (Whitehead, 1993)

- Divorce almost always brings a decline in the standard of living for the mother and children. (Whitehead, 1993)

- One study shows that about 38% of divorced mothers and their children move during the first year after divorce. (Whitehead, 1993)

- Growing up in an intact two-parent family is an important source of advantage for American children. Not only does the intact family protect the child from poverty and economic insecurity; it also provides greater non-economic investments of parental time, attention, and emotional support over the entire life course. (Whitehead, 1993)

© 1998, YouthLight, Inc.

Effects of Divorce on Children

- In 1989, psychologists Judith Wallerstein and Sandra Blakeslee claimed that almost half of the children of divorced parents experience long-term pain, worry, and insecurity that adversely affect their love and work relationships. (Coontz, 1992)

- Researchers who managed to disentangle the effects of divorce itself from the effects of a change in physical location, for example, found that dislocation was much more likely to interfere with school completion than parental separation. (Coontz, 1992)

- Adults in single-parent families tend to spend less time supervising homework or interacting with teachers. Single parents are more likely to get upset and angry when their children receive bad grades. (Coontz, 1992)

- No one suffers more from parental selfishness that children do. A million kids a year have their lives shattered by the divorce of their parents. Half of them will not see the parent who leaves in the first year after divorce. (McManus, 1993)

- By age eighteen, six children out of ten will live in a single-parent family, and half of those absent parents are not required even to provide child support. (McManus, 1993)

- Karl Zinmeister wrote in 1990, "There is a mountain of scientific evidence showing that when families disintegrate, children often end up with intellectual, physical, and emotional scars that persist for life." (McManus, 1993)

- 30% of children who live with never-married mothers have repeated a grade, compared to only 12% of those living with both biological parents. (McManus, 1993)

- Children from single-parent homes are twice as likely to have behavior disorders as children from two-parent homes. (McManus, 1993)

- Crime rates among juveniles are more "associated with family structure than either poverty or race." Neighborhoods with high percentages of single-parent household have high rates of violent crime and burglary. (McManus, 1993)

- Much of the escalating murder rate comes from out-of-wedlock kids being brought up in the streets rather than in homes. (McManus, 1993)

- The National Commission on Children concluded that divorce devastates children, "Depression, trouble getting along with parents and peers, misbehavior stemming from anger and

© 1998, YouthLight, Inc.

declining school performance are common and continue to worsen as they get older." (McManus, 1993)

- From, "Dan Quayle Was Right" by Barbara Dafoe Whitehead (The Atlantic, April, 1993)
  - Children in single-parent families are six times more likely to be poor.
  - A 1988 survey by the National Center for Health Statistics found that children in single-parent families are two to three times as likely as children in two-parent families to have emotional and behavioral problems. They are also more likely to drop out of high school, to get pregnant as teenagers, to abuse drugs, and to be in trouble with the law.
  - Compared with children in intact families, children from disrupted families are at a much higher risk for physical and sexual abuse.
  - Contrary to popular belief, many children do not "bounce back" after divorce. Difficulties that are associated with family breakup often persist into adulthood. Research shows that many children from disrupted families have a harder time achieving intimacy in a relationship, forming a stable marriage, or even holding a steady job.
  - Five years after divorce, more than a third of the children in the study experienced moderate or severe depression.
  - Girls in single-parent homes are also at much greater risk of precocious sexuality, teenage marriage, teenage pregnancy, non-marital birth, and divorce than are girls in two-parent families.
  - According to a Canadian study, preschool children in stepfamilies are 40 times as likely as children in intact families to suffer physical or sexual abuse.
  - Nationally, more that 70% of all juveniles in state reform institutions come from fatherless homes.
  - According to a study by the National Association of Elementary School Principals, 33% of two-parent elementary school students are ranked as high achievers, as compared with 17% of single-parent students.
  - The children in single-parent families are also more likely to be truant or late or to have disciplinary action taken against them.
  - Children in stepfamilies report lower educational aspirations on the part of their parents and lower levels of parental involvement with schoolwork.
  - A 1991 survey by the National Commission on Children showed that the parents in stepfamilies were less likely to be involved in a child's school life, including involvement in extracurricular activities, than either involved in such time-consuming activities as coaching a child's team, accompanying class trips, or helping with school projects.
  - "The great educational tragedy of our time is that many American children are failing in school, not because they are intellectually or physically impaired, but because they are emotionally incapacitated. In schools across the nation principals report a dramatic rise in the aggressive, acting-out behavior characteristics of children, especially boys who live in single-parent families."

- Michael Thompson, a member of Independent School Psychological Consultants and a psychologist who practices in Cambridge, Mass. points out, "We've had a thirty-year epidemic of divorce and a generation of shell-shocked children. We have only begun to understand the long-term effects of having so many busted-up families." (The Atlantic, June, 1991)

© 1998, YouthLight, Inc.

173

- Suicide has tripled among adolescents, from 3.6 deaths per 100,000 in 1960 to 10.2 deaths by 1986 - in the same time that divorces also tripled. A study of state and county data by the National Commission on Children over a 47 year period found that the regions with the highest divorce rates also had the highest suicide rates; in contrast, suicide rates were lowest in those states with the highest rates of church membership. (McManus, 1993)

- Even infants and toddlers can react negatively to divorce with sleep, toilet training and feeding problems. Preschoolers may start hitting or biting their playmates or throwing temper tantrums. Younger school-age kids may react with sadness, school phobia, bed-wetting, or hyperactivity. Meanwhile, older children and teens may feel depressed, lonely, devalued, rejected, hurt, anxious, or ashamed. (Foley and Nechas, 1993)

- Nearly 30 years ago, Daniel Patrick Moynihan observed: "From the wild Irish slums of the 19th century eastern seaboard to the riot-torn suburbs of Los Angeles, there is one unmistakable lesson in American history; a community that allows a large number of young men and women to grow up in broken families, dominated by women, never acquiring male authority . . . that community asks for and gets chaos." (The Atlantic, June 1990)

© 1998, YouthLight, Inc.

What Are Educators Saying?

- Samuel Sava, past head of the National Association of Elementary School Principals, blames the decline of American education on a "parenting deficit." he notes, "It's not better teachers, texts, or curricula that our children need most. . . we will never see lasting school reform until we see parent reform." (Coontz, 1992)

- "Why launch new school reforms when the real key to educational performance is whether a child comes from a two-parent family? Why experiment with a new anti-poverty program when the most important indicator of poverty is whether there are two parents at home?" (Coontz, 1992)

- In a recent article in Education Week, Harold Howe 2nd, former head of the U.S. Office of Education noted:
  - "How anyone could draft the goals of education in this country without an emphasis on families and communities is hard to understand." (Howe was referring to George Bush's educational goals discussed in 1990.)
  - "The first goal of education should be changed to carry the full message initiatives to support and educate families needing help with this responsibility."
  - "Americans must consciously see the family as educational institution and understand that the schools alone cannot provide all the stimulation and guidance young people need to mature successfully."
  - "A Nation At Risk in 1983 sought longer school hours, more tests, and more required subjects but had nothing to say about families until its final few pages, where it delivered a short lecture urging families to take a major interest in the learning of their kids. There was no recognition at all of the very changes in American families in recent years. In effect, that beliwether report assumed that families from Scarsdale and families from Harlem were equally capable of doing more for their youngsters." (Education Week, 2-3-93)

- In 1991, the Carnegie Foundation for the Advancement of Teaching surveyed more than 7,000 kindergarten teachers how well prepared their students were for formal education, focusing especially on physical well-being, social confidence, emotional maturity, language richness, general knowledge, and moral awareness - what we define as the key dimensions of school readiness. The results were deeply troubling. According to teachers, 35% of the nation's children were not ready for school. Even more disturbing, when asked how the readiness of last year's students compared to those enrolled five years ago, 42% of the teachers said that students were more deficient, teachers overwhelming cited, "lack of proficiency in language." In response to the question, "What would most improve the school readiness of children?", the majority said, "Parent education." (Boyer, 1991)

© 1998, YouthLight, Inc.

- "We begin, where we must, with parents. When all is said and done, mothers and fathers are the first and most essential teachers. It's in the home that children must be clothed, fed, and loved. This is the place where life's most basic lessons will be learned. No outside program - no surrogate or substitute arrangement - however well planned or well intended, can replace a supportive family that gives the child emotional security and a rich environment for learning." (Boyer, 1991)

- In 1993, the Metropolitan Life Insurance Company surveyed 1,000 teachers. Highlights from the survey include:
  - 69% of teachers believe that one of the federal government's highest priorities should be programs helping disadvantaged parents work with their children to encourage learning.
  - 86% of teachers feel that parents should be penalized through fines or some other mechanism for allowing their children to be chronically truant.
  - 42% of teachers feel parents should be penalized for refusing to attend parent-teacher conferences.
  (Metlife Survey, 1993)

- In Washington state, the Department of Social and Health Services found that the broadest, most consistent predictors of school failure, substance abuse, delinquency, and adolescent pregnancy were poverty and having parents, whether married or not, who had not graduated from high school. (Coontz, 1992)

- "Teachers find many children emotionally distracted, so upset and preoccupied by the explosive drama of their own family lives that they are unable to concentrate on such mundane matters as multiplication tables." (Whitehead, 1993)

- In response, many schools have turned to therapeutic remediation. A growing proportion of many school budgets is devoted to counseling and other psychological services. (Whitehead, 1993)

© 1998, YouthLight, Inc.

Education Over the Years

1745 The Massachusetts Assembly ordered that any child older than six who did not know the alphabet was to be removed to another family.

1848 Following is a partial list of punishments (lashes) used in a North Carolina school:

Rules of the School	Number of Lashes
....Boys and girls playing together	4
....Fighting	5
....Playing cards at school	10
....Climbing for every foot over 3 feet up a tree	1
....For drinking spirituous liquors at school	8
....Making swings and swinging on them	7
....For wearing long fingernails	2
....For not making a bow when you meet a person	4
....For hollowing and hooping going home	3
....For every word you miss in your Heart Lesson	1

1872 Rules for teachers in St. Augustine, Florida:

* Men teachers may take one evening a week for courting purposes, or two evenings a week if they go to church regularly.
* Women teachers who marry or engage in unseemly conduct will be dismissed.
* Any teacher who smokes, uses liquor in any form, frequents pool or public halls, or gets shaved in a barber shop will give good reason to suspect his worth, intention, integrity, and honesty.

1888 Because children supplied essential farm labor, the school year lasted barely 12 weeks, from thanksgiving through early spring. Men teachers earned an average of $42.43 a month, women made $38.14.

1893 A survey of Brooklyn schools listed 18 classes with 90-100 students. One class had 158.

1959 Following is a "Question & Answer" by A.S. Neill in his book, *Summerhill*.

> Question: "Does correct home rearing counteract the wrong teaching of a school?
> Answer: "In the main, yes. The voice of the home is more powerful than the voice of the school. If the home is free from fear and punishment, the child will not some to believe that the school is right. Parents

© 1998, YouthLight, Inc.

should tell their children what they think of a wrong school. Too often parents have an absurd sense of loyalty to even the most stupid of school teachers."

1972   In their book, *Discipline and the Disruptive Child: A Practical Guide for Elementary Teachers*, authors Karlin and Berger gave teachers this plan to get two students to stop fighting . . . "Use your voice as a weapon. Shriek at the children. Shriek as loudly as you possibly can. Shriek in their ears, if possible. . . .If your shrieking has not helped, try the following procedure: Being very careful of your own safety, if you are able to, try to pull the hair of both combatants. . . ."

© 1998, YouthLight, Inc.

References

Bellah, Robert, <u>The Good Society</u>, 1991, Alfred Knopf, New York.

Boyer, Ernest, <u>Ready To Learn</u>, 1991, Carnegie Foundation, Princeton, NJ.

Bruskin-Goldring Research, EDUCATION WEEK, May 19, 1993.

Caplan, Arthur, Knight Rider, June 24, 1993.

Carnegie Corporation, "A Matter of Time: Risk and Opportunity in the Non-School Hours", 1992, Carnegie Corporation, New York.

Carr, Tom, <u>Keeping Love Alive in the Family</u>, 1992, Professional Press, Chapel Hill, NC.

Carr, Tom, "Student perceptions of non-school hours", 1993, Hillsborough, NC.

Carr, Tom, "What Are the Fears, Worries, Concerns of North Carolina eighth graders?", 1992, Carr Counseling & Consultation, Hillsborough, NC.

Children's Defense Fund, 1991, Annual Report, Washington, D.C.

Coontz, Stephanie, <u>The Way We Never Were</u>, 1992 Basic Books, New York.

Csikszentmihalyi, M. and Larson, R. 1984, <u>Being Adolescent: Conflict and Growth in the Teenage Years</u>, Basic Books, New York.

Csikszentmihalyi, M. and Rochberg-Halton, <u>Meaning of Things</u>, 1981, Cambridge University Press, Cambridge, England.

Fishman, Katherine, "Therapy For Children", THE ATLANTIC, June 1991.

Foley, Denise and Nechas, Eileen, <u>Women's Encyclopedia of Health and Emotional Healing</u>, 1993, Rodale Press, Emmaus, PA.

Glass, J. Conrad, "Death, loss, grief, among middle school children: Implications for the school counselor," Elementary School Guidance & Counseling, volume 26, Dec., 1991.

Goldscheider, Frances, and Waite, Linda, <u>New Families, No Families</u>, 1991, University of California Press, Los Angeles.

© 1998, YouthLight, Inc.

Hopper, G. and Christensen, M. "Identifying and Assisting Depressed Adolescents and Pre-Adolescents," American School Counselor Conference, 1991, Des Moines, Iowa,

Howe, Harold, "We Need Four More National Educational Goals," EDUCATION WEEK, February 3, 1993.

Liebert and Joyce Sprafkin, <u>The Early Window</u>, 1988, Pergamon Press, New York.

Metropolitan Life Survey, "The American Teacher,"1993, Louis Harris, New York.

McManus, Michael, <u>The Marriage Savers</u>, 1993, Zondervan Publishing, Grand Rapids, MI.

Nassar, C., Hodges, P., Ollendick, T., "Self-concept, eating disorders, and dietary patterns in young adolescent girls," School Counselor, Vol. 39, May 1992.

Newman, L. and Buka, S., "Every Child a Learner: Reducing Risks of Learning Impairment During Pregnancy and Infancy," 1990, Education Commission of the States, Denver.

Parker, Harvey, <u>The ADD Hyperactivity Handbook for Schools</u>, 1992, Impact Publications, Plantation, FL.

Pelton, L., "Child Abuse and Neglect: The Myth of Classlessness," American Journal of Orthopsychiatry, Vol. 48, 1978.

Radecki, D., "Cartoon Report", April 1991, National Coalition of Television Violence, Champaign, IL.

Simon, Paul, "Reducing Violence on Television," EDUCATION WEEK, October 4, , 1989.

Stinnet, N. and DeFrain, J., <u>Secrets of Strong Families</u>, 1986, Little and Brown, Boston.

Taras, H. et al, "Children's television viewing habits and the family environment," Journal of Diseases of Children, Vol. 144, March 1990.

Timmer, S., 1985, "How Children Use Time," University of Michigan, Ann Arbor.

USA TODAY, April 20, 1993

USA TODAY, May 3, 1990.

USA TODAY, June 8, 1993

USA TODAY, June 16, 1993

Whitehead, Barbara, "Dan Quayle Was Right.", THE ATLANTIC, April 1993.

© 1998, YouthLight, Inc.

Will, George, Washington Post, June 15, 1993.

Wilson, J. and Blocher, L. "The counselor's role in assisting children of alcoholics." Elementary School Guidance and Counseling, Vol. 25, Dec. 1990.

Woodside, M. "Children of Alcoholics: A Report to the Governor", 1992, Children of Alcoholics Foundations.

Zinsmeister, Karl, "Growing Up Scared, THE ATLANTIC, June 1990.

Books

Affective Enterprises (1987). <u>Friendship</u>. Callahan, FL.

Borba, M. and Borba, C. (1978). <u>Self-Esteem: A Classroom Affair.</u> Harper and Row.

Borba, M. (1989). <u>Esteem Builders,</u> Jalmar Press, California, 1989.

Brun, J., (1992). <u>They can, but they don't: Helping students overcome work inhibition.</u> New York: Viking.

Frey, Di. and C. Jesse Carlock, <u>Enhancing Self-Esteem.</u> Accelerated Development Inc., 1989 (1-800-222-1166).

From the editors of Group Publishing, <u>Group Growers</u>. Thom Schultz Publications, Inc. 1988.

Graves, F. (1989). <u>Staff Development Workshop</u>. Richland School District One, Columbia, SC

Hallinan, P.K. <u>I'm Glad to be Me.</u> Children's Press, Chicago, 1977.

Kreidler, W.J. (1984). <u>Creative Conflict Resolution</u>. Glenview, IL: Scott, Foresman, and Company.

Landy, L. (1988). <u>Child Support (through small group counseling)</u>. Mount Dora, FL: Kidsrights.

Lesesne, T. (1986). <u>I'm Special</u>. Charlotte, NC: The Drug Education Center.

Lions-Quest, (1989). <u>Training Curriculum: Skills for Growing</u>. Rock Hill, SC: Quest International.

Muntean, Michaela. <u>The Little Engine That Could.</u> Platt and Munk Publishers, 1988.

© 1998, YouthLight, Inc.

Myrick, R.D. (1987). <u>Developmental Guidance and Counseling: A Practical Approach</u>. Minneapolis, MN: Educational Media Corporation.

Palmer, P. (1977). <u>The Mouse, Monster, and Me.</u> San Luis Obispo, CA: Impact Publishers

Phillips, Deborah, <u>How to Give your Child a Great Self-Esteem.</u> Random House, 1989.

<u>Pumsy, in Pursuit of Excellence</u> and <u>Pumsy, Bright Beginnings.</u> Timberline Press, (P.O. Box 70187, Eugene, Oregon, 97401).

Smith, S. and Walter, G. <u>Four Steps to Making Friends Training Manual</u>. Rock Hill, SC: Winthrop College.

Weinstein, M. and Goodman, J. (1980). <u>Playfair</u>. San Luis Obispo, CA: Impact Publishers.

Journals

Adams, W. (1989). The fruit basket. <u>PIC (Practical Ideas for Counselors)</u>, 2, 6-7.

Cooper, J. and Martenz, J. (1989). Understanding differences, <u>PIC (Practical Ideas for Counselors)</u>, 2, 3-4.

Sacharow-Nayowith, R. (1989). Prejudice, <u>PIC (Practical Ideas for Counselors)</u>, 2, 3-4.

Other Suggested Resources

(Note: this list is not comprehensive or exhaustive. It represents materials on display, favorite materials used by the authors, and a few selected others.)

<u>Raising Self-Reliant Children In a Self Indulgent World</u>
 By H. Stephen Glenn and Jane Nelson
 Prima Publishing & Communications
 P.O. Box 1260 SR
 Rockling, CA 95677
 (916) 624-5718

<u>Five Cries of Parents: New Help for Families on the Issues that Trouble Them Most</u>
 By Merton P. Strommen & A. Irene Strommen
 Harper & Row Publishers, Inc.
 10 East 53rd Street
 New York, NY 10022
<u>How Children Fail</u>
 By John Holt
 Dell Publishing Co., Inc.
 750 Third Avenue, New York, NY 10017

© 1998, YouthLight, Inc.

Control Theory in the Classroom
    By William Glasser, M.D.
    Harper & Row, Publishers, Inc.
    10 East 53rd St., New York, NY 10022

Control Theory: A New Explanation of How We Control Our Lives
    By William Glasser, M.D.
    Harper & Row, Publishers, Inc.
    10 East 53rd St., New York, NY 10022

Games People Play
    By Eric Berne, M.D.
    Grove Press, Inc.
    New York, NY

Depression in Young People
    Edited by M. Rutler, C.E. Izard, & P.B. Read
    The Guilford Press
    200 Park Avenue South
    New York, NY 10003

The Acting-Out Child: Coping with Classroom Disruption
    By Hill M. Walker
    Allyn and Bacon, Inc.
    470 Atlantic Avenue
    Boston, MA 02210

Coping with Difficult People
    By Robert M. Bramson
    Doubleday
    666 Fifth Avenue
    New York, NY 10103

Winning Children Over: A Manual for Teachers, Counselors, Principals and Parents
    By Francis X. Walton & Robert L. Powers
    Adlerian Childcare Books
    Box 210206
    Columbia, SC 29221

Between Parent & Teenager
    By Haim Ginott
    Macmillan Publishing Company
    866 Third Avenue
    New York, NY 10022
Between Teacher and Child
    By Haim Ginott
    Avon Books
    105 Madison Avenue
    New York, NY 10016

© 1998, YouthLight, Inc.

People Making

By Virginia Satir
Science and Behavior Books, Inc.
Palo Alto, CA

All Grown Up and No Place to Go The Hurried Child Children and Adolescents

By David Elkind
Alfred A. Knopf, Inc.
New York, NY

How to Help Children with Common Problems

Schaefer, C.E., Millman, H.L.
The Mosby Press
The C.V. Mosby Company
11830 Westline Industrial Drive
St. Louis, MO 63141

Positive Discipline

By Jane Nelsen
Ballentine Books
Random House, Inc.
New York, NY

Discipline without Tears

By Rudolf Dreikurs and Cassel, Pearl
E.P. Dutton, Inc.
2 Park Avenue
New York, NY 10016

Teaching/Discipline

By Madsen, C.H., Madson, C.K.
Allyn & Bacon, Inc.
470 Atlantic Avenue
Boston, MA

Discipline and the Disruptive Child

By Kaslin, M., and Berger, R.
Parker Publishing Company, Inc.
West Nyack, NY

Children: The Challenge

By Dreikurs, R.
E.P. Dulton
2 Park Avenue
New York, NY 10016

© 1998, YouthLight, Inc.

Six Point Plan for Raising Happy, Healthy Children
  By Rosemond, John
  Anderson and McNeel, A Universal Press Syndicate Company
  4900 Main Street
  Kansas City, MO 64122

Dare to Discipline The Strong-Willed Child
  By Dobson, James
  Tyndale House Publishers, Inc.
  Wheaton, Illinois 60187

Winning the Homework War
  By Levine, F.M. and Anesko, K.M.
  Prentiss-Hall Press
  A Division of Session and Sebustu, Inc.
  Gulf and Western Building
  One Gulf and Western Place
  New York, NY 10023

How to Talk So Kids Will Listen and Listen So Kids Will Talk
  By Faber, Adele and Elaine Mozlisk
  Avon Books, A Division of The Hearst Corporation
  105 Madison Avenue
  New York, NY 10016

Feeling Good About Me
  By Kenneth Morrison and Monica Thompson
  Educational Media Corporation
  P.O. Box 21311
  Minneapolis, Minnesota 55421

Your Child's Self-Esteem
  By Dorothy Cookville Briggs
  A Dolphin Book
  Bantam Doubleday Dell Publishing Co., Inc.
  666 Fifth Avenue. New York, NY 10103

The Other Side of the Report Card
  By Larry Chase
  Paperbacks for Educators
  1240 Ridge Road
  Ballwin, Missouri 63021
  (800) 227-2591   MO (314) 227-2590

100 Ways to Enhance Self-Concept in the Classroom
  By Jack Canfield and Harold Wells
  Prentiss Hall, Inc.
  Englewood Cliffs, NJ

© 1998, YouthLight, Inc.

<u>Life 101</u>
By John Roger, Peter McWilliams
Prelude Press
8165 Mannix Drive
Los Angeles, CA 90046

<u>Helping Children Choose</u>
By George M. Schuncke and Susan Lowell Krogh
Scott, Foresman, and Company
Glenview, Illinois 60025

<u>Energizers and Icebreakers</u>
By Elizabeth S. Foster
Educational Media Corporation
P.O. Box 21311
Minneapolis, Minnesota 55421

<u>Substance Abuse Prevention Activities for Elementary Children</u>
By Timothy A. Gerne, Jr. , Patrick J. Gerne
Prentice-Hall Inc.
Englewood Cliffs, NJ

<u>How to Talk to Children about Really Important Things</u>
By Charles E. Shaefer
Paperbacks for Educators
Washington, Missouri 63090
(800) 227-2591   (314) 239-1999

<u>Games Children Should Play</u>
By Mary K. Cihak, Barbara J. Heron
Paperbacks for Educators
1240 Ridge Rd.
Ballwin, Baldwin, MO 63021

<u>Belonging</u>
By Jayne Devencenzi and Susan Pendergast
2960 Hawk Hill Lane
San Luis Obispo CA 95401

<u>Helping Children Cope with Separation and Loss</u>
By Claudia L. Jewett
The Harvard Common Press, Inc.
535 Albany Street
Boston, MA 02118

<u>A Survival Guide for the Elementary/Middle School Counselor</u>
By John J. Schmidt
The Center for Applied Research in Education, Inc.
Business Information Publishing Div.
West Nyack, NY 10995

© 1998, YouthLight, Inc.

Counseling Young Students at Risk
    By Jeanne C. Bleur and Penny A. Schrieber
    ERU Counseling and Personnel Services Clearinghouse
    2108 School of Education
    The University of Michigan
    Ann Arbor, Michigan 48109-1259

The Compassionate School
    By Gertrude Morrow
    Prentiss-Hall, Inc.
    Englewood Cliffs, NJ

Learning to Care
    By Norma Deitch Fishback
    Paperbacks for Educators
    1240 Ridge Road
    Ballwin, Missouri 63021
    (800) 227-2591   MO (314) 227-2590

© 1998, YouthLight, Inc.

Free Catalogs of Materials Available on Related Topics

Sunburst Communications
Fax: 914-747-4109 Toll Free: 800-431-1934
101Castlenton St.
P.O. Box 100
Pleasantville, NY 10570-0040

Childswork/Childsplay
100 Plaza Dr.
Secausus, NJ 07094
1-800-962-1141

Mar-co Products, Inc.
1443 Old York Road
Warminster, PA 18974
1-800-448-2197

Negotiation Institute Inc.
341 Madison Avenue, 20th Floor
New York, NY 10017-3705
(212) 986-5555 FAX: (212) 599-3077

Kidsrights
10100 Park Cedar Drive
Charlotte, NC 28210
1-800-892-KIDS
(704) 541-0100 FAX: 704-541-0113

NIMCO. INC.
102 Hwy. 81 N.
P.O. Box 9
Calhoun, KY 42327-009
1-800-962-6662 FAX: 502-273-5844

American Guidance Service
4201 Woodland Road
P.O. Box 99
Circle Pines, MN 55014-1796
1-800-328-2560 FAX: 612-786-9077

© 1998, YouthLight, Inc.

National School Products
10 East Broadway
Maryville, TN 37081-37804
(615) 984-3960
1-800-627-9393 FAX: 1-800-289-3960

Ready Reference Press
P.O. Box 5249
Santa Monica, CA 90409
1-800-424-5627 FAX: 1-310-475-4895

Paperbacks for Educators
426 West Front Street
Washington, MO 63090
1-800-227-2591
(314) 239-1999 FAX: 314-239-4515

J. Weston Walch, Publisher
321 Valley Street
P.O. Box 658
Portland, Maine 04104-0658
1-800-341-6094 FAX: 1-207-772-3105

CFKR Career Marerials, Inc.
11860 Kemper Road, Unit 7
Auburn, CA 95603
1-800-525-5626 FAX: 916-889-0433

Social Studies School Service
10200 Jefferson Blvd. Room M011
P.O. Box 802
Culver City, CA 90232-0802
1-800-421-4246 FAX: 310-839-2249

Education Media Corporation
4256 Central Ave.
Minneapolis, MN 55421-0311
1-800-966-3382

© 1998, YouthLight, Inc.

About the Authors

Robert P. Bowman, Ph.D., is a former teacher, counselor, and professional entertainer who makes each of his presentations extremely practical and fun. Dr. Bowman is currently an Associate Professor in the Department of Educational Psychology at the University of South Carolina. He has written 15 nationally recognized books and programs that relate to motivating students from grades K-12.

Tom Carr, M.S., is a much sought-after consultant who has presented more than a hundred workshops to educators and other professional groups. He is a unique presenter whose workshops are "high energy," entertaining, and impelling. Participants leave his workshops feeling energized and filled with useful ideas they can take back to their schools and use immediately. Tom is the author of the book, *Keeping Love Alive in the Family* which is a practical guide to building a more harmonious family life. In addition, Tom has written, *150 Ways to Keep Your Lover, A Parents Blueprint,* and *Monday Morning Messages* along with several professional articles for educators and parents.

Kathy Cooper, M.S.W., is known as an outstanding presenter with an extensive collection of creative and useful strategies for working with many different types of difficult youth. People leave her workshops feeling "energized" and "full of many fresh ideas and strategies." Kathy has worked with difficult youth as a social worker and school counselor where she has been developing strategies that lead to real-and-lasting positive changes in the attitudes, beliefs, and behaviors of difficult students. She is the co-author of *Power Play* and *Quality Times for Quality Kids.*

Ron Miles, Ph.D., is an inspirational speaker and workshop leader who has presented motivaional workshops for educators around the United States. Participants leave his workshops with an extensive collection of practical strategies and activities they can use with students. He is especially known for his work with alternative approaches for "cutting through" to difficult youth. Ron is the Director of Guidance for an inner-city school district and Adjunct Professor in the Department of Educational Psychology at the University of South Carolina. He has won several state and national awards for his dedication to helping youth. In 1998 he was named National Guidance Administrator of the Year by the American School Counselor Association.

© 1998, YouthLight, Inc.